JAMES MCNEILL WHISTLER

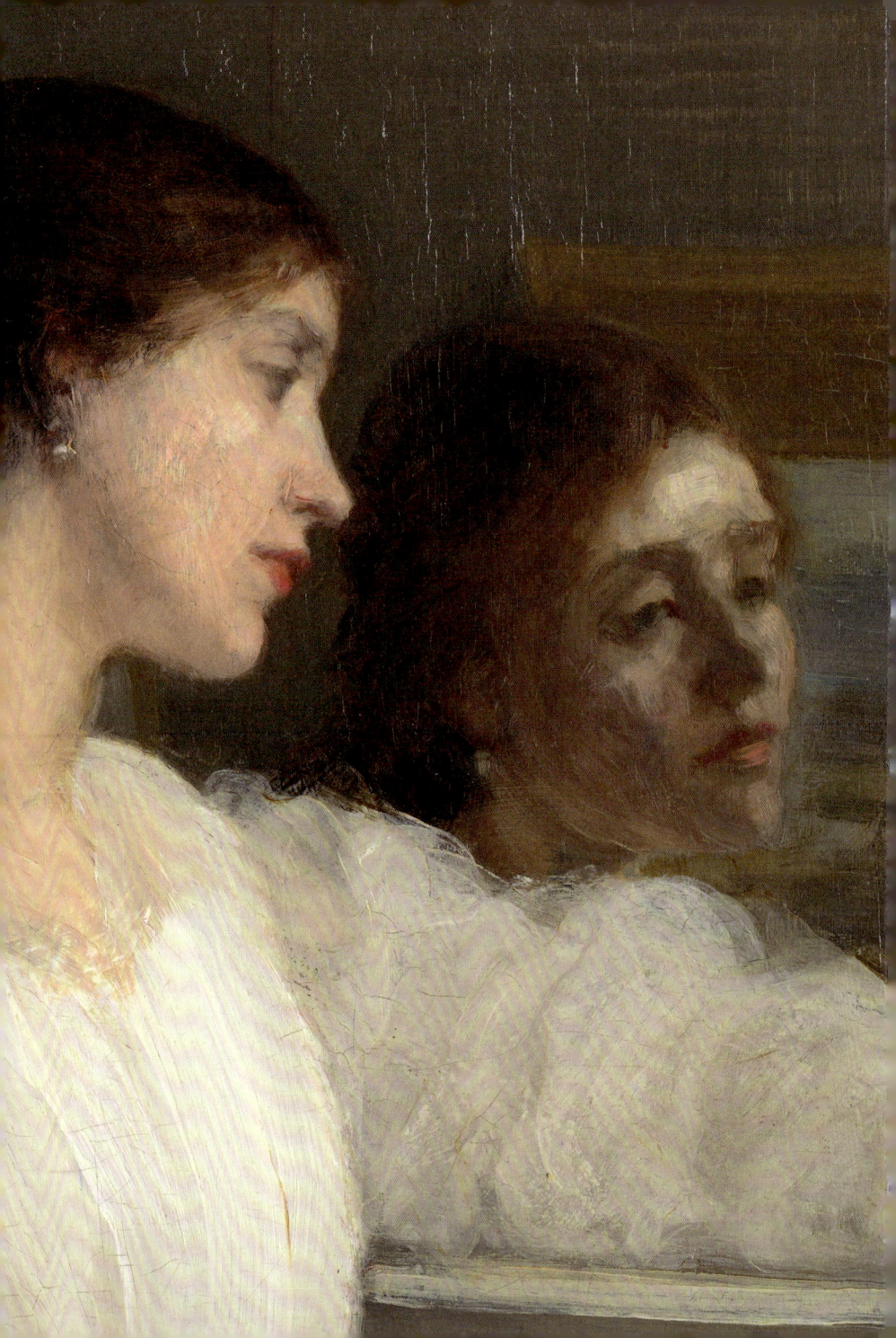

JAMES MCNEILL WHISTLER

JAMES FINCH

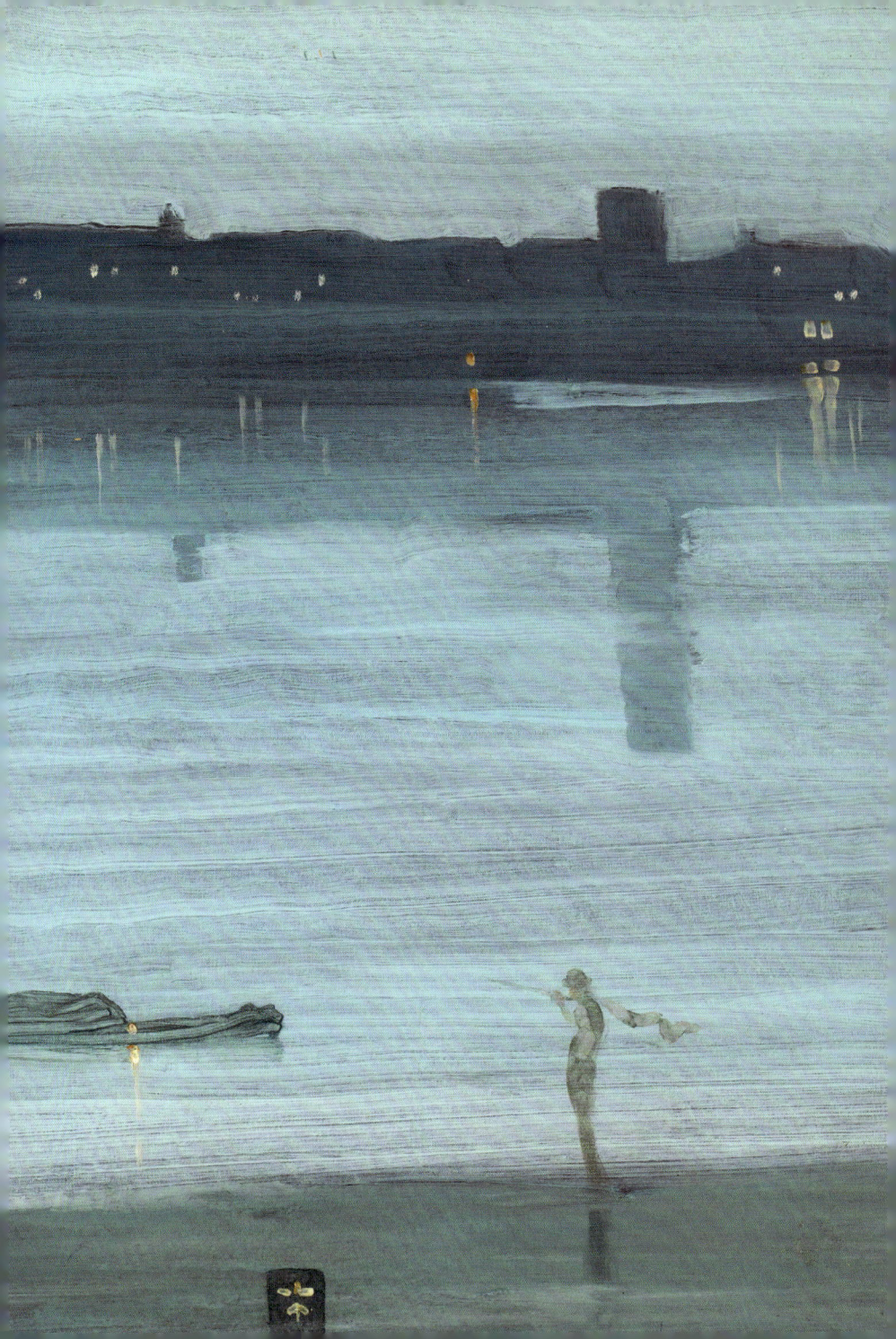

NOCTURNES

One afternoon in August 1871, James McNeill Whistler and his mother Anna took a steamer along the Thames from their home in Chelsea to visit friends. Returning home later that day, Whistler was inspired to paint by the sight of 'the river in a glow of rare transparency'. Anna watched him paint, later recalling: 'I was so fascinated I hung over his magic touches till the bright moon faced us from his window – & I exclaimed Oh Jemie dear it is yet light enough for you to see to make this a moonlight picture of the Thames.'[1]

The resulting painting, *Nocturne: Blue and Silver – Chelsea 1871* (opposite), was the first of a series of pictures in which Whistler sought to evoke the atmosphere of the Thames by night, when it was empty of its bustling daytime activity.[2] The painting is largely composed of horizontal bands of colour in subtly differentiated shades of blue. The buildings of the Chelsea riverside can be seen in silhouette, dotted with yellow lights and reflected in the water; in the foreground, a long barge stretches out horizontally and a spectral figure stands on the shore. Whistler worked in oil paint as if it were watercolour, exploiting its liquidity. He painted with what he called his 'sauce', a runny mixture including copal resin, turpentine and linseed oil, which he washed onto the canvas, lightening and darkening it as he progressed. Canvases were placed flat to keep the 'sauce' from running off.

Whistler named these paintings 'nocturnes' (after a genre of quiet piano composition evoking the night, favoured by composers such as Chopin) at the suggestion of his patron, the shipowner Frederick Richards Leyland (p.48).[3] Following the critic Walter Pater, who wrote in 1869 that 'all art aspires to the condition of music', Whistler frequently borrowed musical terminology for his titles, naming other works 'symphonies' or 'harmonies' (a debt later repaid when Whistler's titles inspired that of George Gershwin's 1924 composition *Rhapsody in Blue*). This was a way for Whistler to distinguish his works from topographical depictions. They were, as he later explained, 'an arrangement of line, form, and colour first'.[4]

These paintings also explored the subjective experience of place and the workings of memory. Whistler would often have himself rowed out on the river by his neighbours, the aspiring artists Henry and Walter Greaves, and spend hours contemplating his surroundings before painting from memory back in his studio. His nocturnes were literally 'impressionist'

Nocturne: Blue and Silver – Chelsea 1871
Oil paint on wood
50.2 × 60.8

– impressions of a place. No one had painted London like this before. As Whistler later described it, 'when the evening mist clothes the riverside with poetry, as with a veil – and the poor buildings lose themselves in the dim sky – and the tall chimneys become campanile … Nature, who for once, has sung in tune, sings her exquisite song to the Artist alone.'[5] Whistler was her audience.

THE MAKING OF AN ARTIST

Whistler only settled in London as an adult, having already travelled widely in his youth. He was born in Lowell, Massachusetts, in 1834, the child of Major George Washington Whistler and Anna Matilda McNeill, who hailed from Indiana and North Carolina respectively. After his father, an engineer, was hired to oversee construction of a railway line from St Petersburg to Moscow, Whistler lived in Russia for several years, receiving his earliest artistic education at the Imperial Academy of Fine Arts in St Petersburg. He followed in his father's footsteps by enrolling at the United States Military Academy at West Point in 1851, but proved an indifferent student and was discharged owing to poor grades. Throughout his life, however, he enjoyed referring to himself as a 'West Point man'. Whistler's artistic gifts (and contacts) led to him gaining a position with the US Coast and Geodetic Survey in Washington, DC, where he drew maps and topographical views. Here Whistler also learned the art of etching, which he went on to practise with a rare virtuosity. His impatience with the discipline of topography is evident in one plate from this period, in which, unable to confine himself to the government requirements, he etched several figures alongside the coastal profile including 'a battered French soldier' and 'a bearded monk in an elaborate cowl' (p.26).[6] Within months Whistler left the survey, having resolved to become an artist.

In 1855, barely a year later, the twenty-one-year-old Whistler moved to Paris, the centre of the European art world, where he spent three and a half years taking drawing classes, making copies of artworks and working in the studio of the history painter Charles Gleyre. More importantly perhaps, he befriended artists including Henri Fantin-Latour and Alphonse Legros (with whom he formed a group, the Société des Trois), and the realist painter Gustave Courbet. Whistler's major work of the period was his first set of etchings: the skills he had developed in Washington turned to more personal ends. First

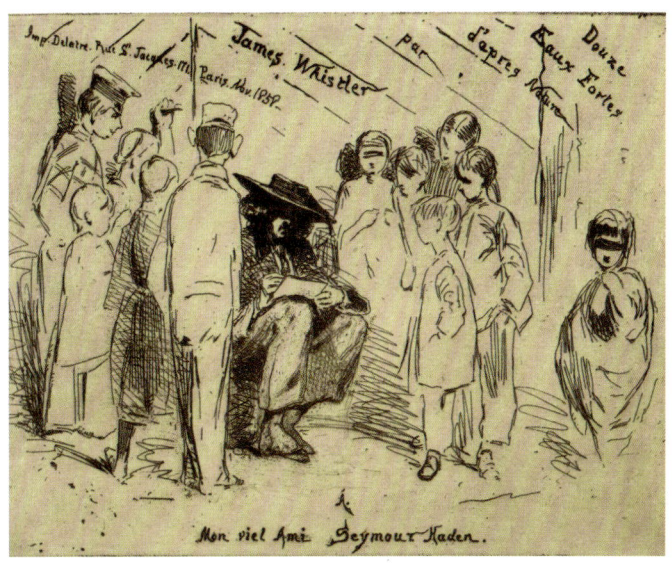

issued in Paris in 1858, *Douze Eaux Fortes d'après Nature* ('Twelve Etchings from Nature', popularly known as the 'French Set') showcased Whistler's breadth. The set comprised portraits, landscapes (showing his particular interest in the built environment) and genre scenes depicting working interiors. While Whistler's style and artistic vocabulary evolved in later years, he continued to favour these genres throughout his career. The set also introduced Whistler as a personality: the title-page to the set shows the artist surrounded by a group of children admiringly watching him work. The dandyish Whistler, with his characteristic wide-brimmed hat, would become almost as immediately recognisable as his art.

The French Set was dedicated ('a mon vieil ami') to Francis Seymour Haden, the English physician and artist who in 1847 had married Whistler's half-sister Deborah. The couple's presence in London was a key factor in Whistler's decision to move to the city in 1859, along with the financial and artistic opportunities he anticipated finding there. Haden was also a catalyst for Whistler's career: a printmaker in his own right and a notable collector, particularly of Rembrandt etchings, he was able to help Whistler navigate London's artistic circles. The men sometimes etched together, and Haden installed a press in his house so they could pull prints themselves (a second edition of the French Set was published from Haden's house).[7]

The Title Page for 'Douze Eaux Fortes d'après Nature' 1858
Etching on paper
11.2 × 14.7

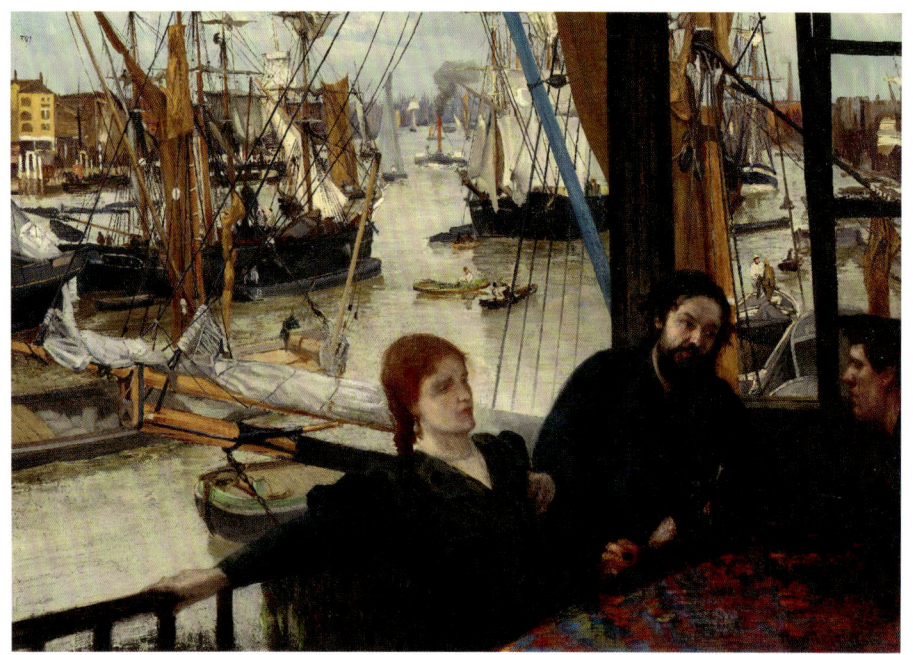

The bourgeois gentility of the Hadens' Chelsea home was the subject of Whistler's breakthrough painting *At the Piano* 1858–9 (pp.30–1), in which Deborah plays the piano while her daughter Annie watches. The solemnity of the work (both figures are dressed in mourning) provides an emotional counterweight to its formal harmony. With this painting Whistler announced himself to the London art world: when it was exhibited at the Royal Academy of Arts in 1860, the painter John Everett Millais pronounced it 'the finest piece of colour that has been on the walls of the Royal Academy for years'.[8]

LONDON

In London, Whistler continued the project of depicting working-class people and environments that he had initiated in the French Set. He took rooms in Wapping, a riverside district near the London docks which the American novelist Nathaniel Hawthorne described as 'a cold and torpid neighbourhood, mean, shabby, and unpicturesque, both as to its buildings and inhabitants'.[9] There, 'among a beastly set of cads and every possible annoyance and misery', Whistler worked on a set of etchings later published as *A Series of Sixteen Etchings of Scenes on the Thames* (or 'The Thames Set').[10] London being the largest port in Europe, the Pool of London heaved with activity, but Whistler was drawn less to the spectacle of commerce than to the sprawl of dilapidated warehouses, barges, decaying wharves, and sailors and longshoremen by the river's edge. The prints depict this environment in vivid detail: an etching of a lime burner, for instance, was exhibited not simply under a generic title but as a portrait of 'w. Jones, Lime-burner, Thames Street' (p.33). The poet and critic Charles Baudelaire, whose seminal text 'The Painter of Modern Life' is contemporary with these etchings, wrote admiringly of them in an 1862 article:

> Very recently a young American artist, м. Whistler,
> was showing at the Galerie Martinet a series of etchings,
> subtle, as alive as improvisation or inspiration itself,
> representing the banks of the Thames; wonderful
> jumbles of rigging, yard-arms, and cables; a chaos
> of mist, of furnaces and corkscrews of smoke; profound
> and complicated poetry of a vast capital city.[11]

The culmination of this period was a painting, *Wapping*, begun in 1860 but not finished until 1864 (opposite). The view is from the balcony of the Angel Inn in Rotherhithe (pubs and taverns appear frequently in Whistler's work), with the buildings of Wapping visible across the river on the left. The teeming river traffic, from rowboats to tall ships, provides the backdrop for three figures seated on the balcony. 'I assure you that I have never attempted such a difficult subject', Whistler wrote to Fantin-Latour, and *Wapping* had to be painted and repainted numerous times before the artist was happy with it.[12] By this time, Whistler was moving away from realism and modern life subjects.Writing to Fantin-Latour about progress on *Wapping*, Whistler implored him 'Hush! Not a word to Courbet', acknowledging the proximity to Courbet's subject matter,[13] but by 1867 he was distancing himself from the realism of his earlier work: 'Courbet! and his influence was odious! ... That damned Realism made an *immediate* appeal to my vanity as a painter! and mocking all tradition cried out loud, with all the confidence of ignorance, "Long live Nature!!"'[14]

Having often stayed with Deborah and Haden in Chelsea, Whistler took the first of many addresses of his own in the area in 1862. The Thames between Westminster and Battersea then became his favoured subject matter. Two of his first paintings of this stretch, *The Last of Old Westminster* 1862 (p.35) and *Brown and Silver: Old Battersea Bridge* 1859–63 (p.34), show how Whistler, an engineer's son, was captivated by the bridges spanning the Thames.

The Last of Old Westminster shows Whistler in his realist mode – painting as news (Whistler didn't wait for the completion of the new Westminster Bridge but showed its final stages of construction) – while *Brown and Silver*, in spite of the group of figures by the shore and the carriages crossing the old wooden bridge, already summons the gauzy atmosphere of the nocturnes to come. He went on to make not only river landscapes but also many etchings, lithographs and water-colours of the streets, shops and people of Chelsea. He resided in Chelsea for most of his adult life, and became one of the area's most celebrated figures. A statue of the artist at Cheyne Walk, erected in 2005, now looks out onto the river.

JOANNA HIFFERNAN

The female figure in *Wapping* was modelled by Joanna Hiffernan, an Irish woman who sat for many of Whistler's paintings and prints during the 1860s, a period in which his style evolved rapidly. She was also Whistler's partner during this time. Hiffernan first modelled for Whistler's *Symphony in White, No.1: The White Girl* (opposite) in Paris in the winter of 1861; exhibited in 1862, the painting presaged the direction his work was to take. Standing on a wolfskin rug, Hiffernan wears a simple white cambric dress, similar in style to the aesthetic popularised by Jane Morris among others, and free of the rigid structure of Victorian formal dress. Similarly, the painting slips the constraints of Victorian realism: the composition is arresting but enigmatic, providing no narrative or external referent. When the *Athenaeum* magazine suggested it illustrated Wilkie Collins's 1860 novel *The Woman in White*, Whistler refuted this in a letter clarifying that 'my painting represents a girl dressed in white standing in front of a white curtain'.[15] The painting was rejected by the Royal Academy in 1862, leading Whistler to wage 'open war on the Academy'.[16] It was, however, admired by Baudelaire and others when shown in Paris at the Salon des Refusés the following year, prompting Fantin-Latour to declare to his friend: 'Now you are famous.'[17]

Hiffernan next modelled for *Symphony in White, No.2: The Little White Girl* 1864 (p.39), one of several works demonstrating the influence of Japanese and Chinese art on Whistler. Her face

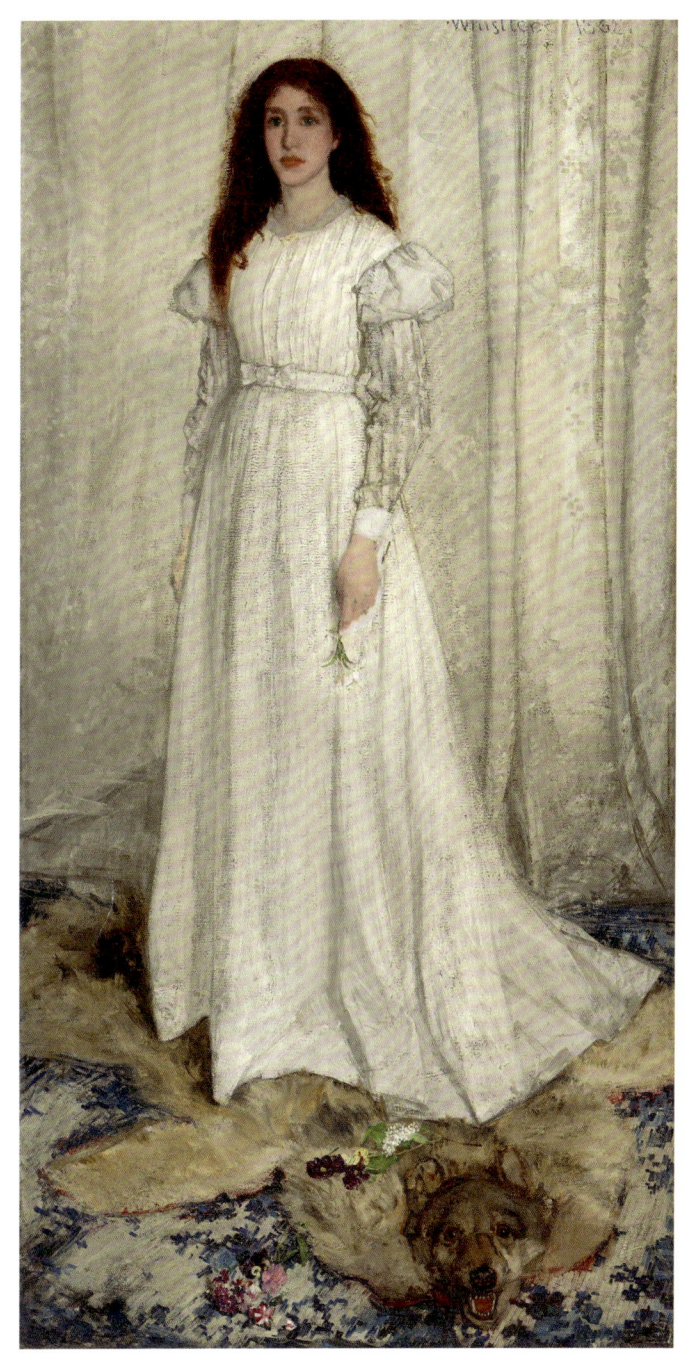

Symphony in White, No.1:
The White Girl 1861–3,
further additions made
in 1872
Oil paint on canvas
213 × 107.9

reflected in a mirror, Hiffernan holds a fan decorated with Utagawa Hiroshige's 1857 print *The Banks of the Sumida River*, while she contemplates a porcelain vase on a mantelpiece. The longstanding Japanese embargo on foreign shipping had been gradually lifted, and Japanese prints and decorative art objects were becoming available in Europe.[18] Whistler and many other artists, including his Chelsea neighbour Dante Gabriel Rossetti, competed to acquire valuable objects such as porcelain, which would then appear in their paintings. Solidifying Whistler's links with aestheticism, the poet Algernon Swinburne wrote a poem in response to *The Little White Girl*, 'Before the Mirror' (1865), which Whistler then printed and pasted on the frame before the work was sent to the Royal Academy for exhibition. While not a description of the painting, Swinburne's poem seems to be written from the perspective of the person depicted, and begins: 'Come snow, come wind or thunder high up in air, / I watch my face, and wonder at my bright hair.'[19]

Hiffernan also modelled for *Purple and Rose: The Lange Leizen of the Six Marks* 1864 (p.42), as a porcelain dealer painting a pot, and *Symphony in White, No.3* 1865–7 (pp.40–1), in which (wearing the same dress as in *The Little White Girl*) she reclines on a sofa alongside a second figure, modelled by Milly Jones. In the foreground is a Chinese rug borrowed from Rossetti.[20] The completion of *Symphony in White* coincided with Whistler's work on a frieze of figures commissioned by Leyland, with which this painting shares a horizontal disposition of figures. 'Oh! how I wish I had been a pupil of Ingres!' Whistler wrote the year he finished *Symphony in White*,[21] and alongside the continuing influence of Japanese and Chinese art the painting reflects an interest in the restraint of classicism.

FAMILY MATTERS

Whistler and Hiffernan separated in 1866, much of which year the artist spent in Chile. In one of the most extraordinary episodes of his career he became involved in a scheme to deliver torpedoes to the coastal city of Valparaíso, in order to relieve the Spanish naval blockade of the city. In the end, the bombardment of Valparaíso and the departure of the Spanish fleet took place long before the armaments arrived, but Whistler (who travelled separately from the ship carrying the torpedoes) spent several months in South America, painting several works including *Crepuscule in Flesh Colour and*

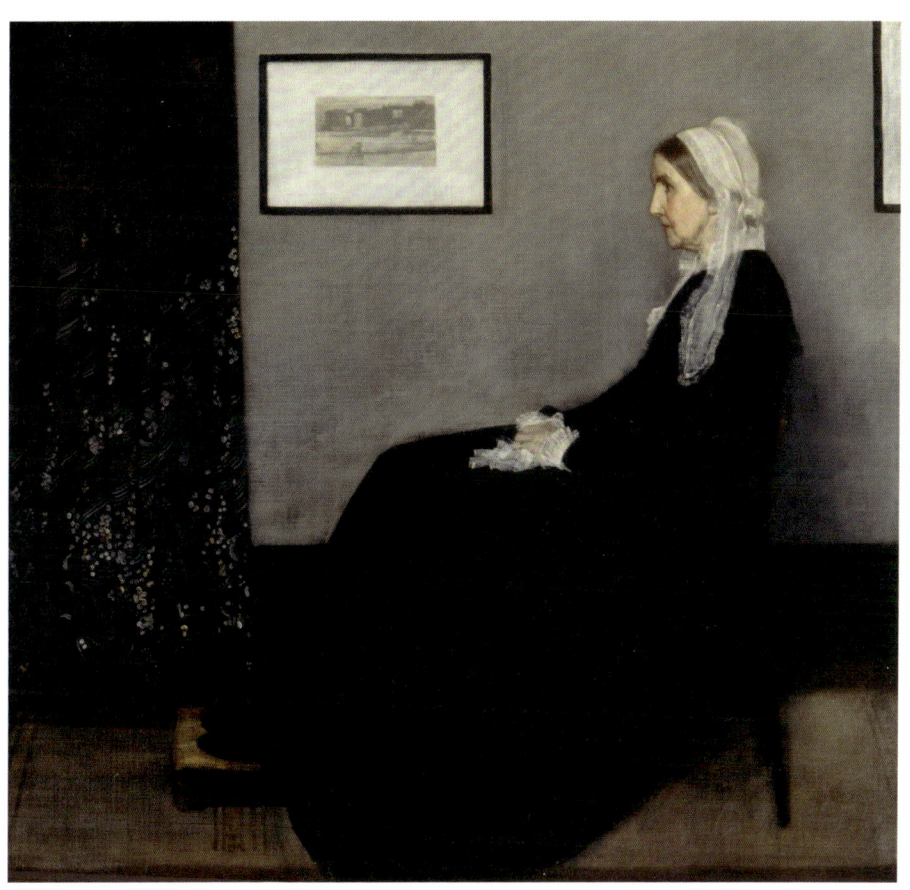

Arrangement in Grey and Black: Portrait of the Painter's Mother
1871
Oil paint on canvas
144.3 × 162.5

Green: Valparaíso 1866 (p.47). The Valparaíso mission had come about through Whistler's brother William, and specifically through his Confederate contacts. William had been a surgeon in the Confederate army, and travelled to London in 1865 after he was granted a furlough. Numerous expatriate Confederates had made their homes in London, and some were now acting as advisers or mercenaries for foreign governments. For both Whistler and the ex-Confederates he accompanied to Chile, the motivation for the mission was primarily financial, although Whistler's Valparaíso paintings proved to be an artistic breakthrough.

His brother's arrival in London made up somewhat for the increasingly strained relationship between Whistler and the Hadens, including Francis Haden's coldness towards

Joanna, and the two men's growing artistic rivalry. Their relationship was shattered in 1867 when Whistler pushed Haden through a glass window following an argument. The break between Whistler and Haden, in turn, created tensions within the family which lasted long afterwards.

Whistler's mother Anna was also installed in London by this time, having moved from Richmond, Virginia (where she had been caring for William's wife) during the American Civil War. (Whistler, for his part, also felt an emotional, familial allegiance to the South, and held racist views.) A devout Christian whose religious piety and rigid morals contrasted with those of her bohemian son, Anna nonetheless lived with Whistler in Chelsea for eleven years before moving to Hastings on doctor's advice in 1875. In 1871 she sat for what has become Whistler's best-known painting, *Arrangement in Grey and Black: Portrait of the Painter's Mother* (p.13). The painting shows Anna seated – standing proved too tiring – in Whistler's Chelsea studio, with his etching *Black Lion Wharf* 1859 (p.32) hanging on the wall behind her, and an intricately patterned curtain to her right. The portrait was the first work which Whistler titled an 'arrangement', privileging the predominant colours of grey and black over the identity of the sitter. The painting was received coolly when first exhibited at the Royal Academy, and Whistler mused sardonically that adding 'a glass of sherry and the Bible' might have made it more successful with a public accustomed to pictures full of objects suggesting narrative and symbolism. However, it has gone on to become an icon, referenced everywhere from postage stamps to *The Simpsons*.[22]

MAKING ARRANGEMENTS

The title of 'arrangement' that Whistler attached to the portrait of his mother not only underlined his attention to composition, but made explicit something that was central to his artistic identity more broadly. The same meticulous approach Whistler took to composing his paintings was matched by his care in all aspects of displaying them. He devised a butterfly motif (based on his initials) which served not only as a signature but as a distinct visual element, and designed and decorated his frames.

The dense 'salon hang' characteristic of the Royal Academy was increasingly incompatible with Whistler's own ideals for the display of his art, and in 1874 he held the first of several one-man shows in London which allowed him to display his work as he saw fit. Whistler leased a gallery and painted the

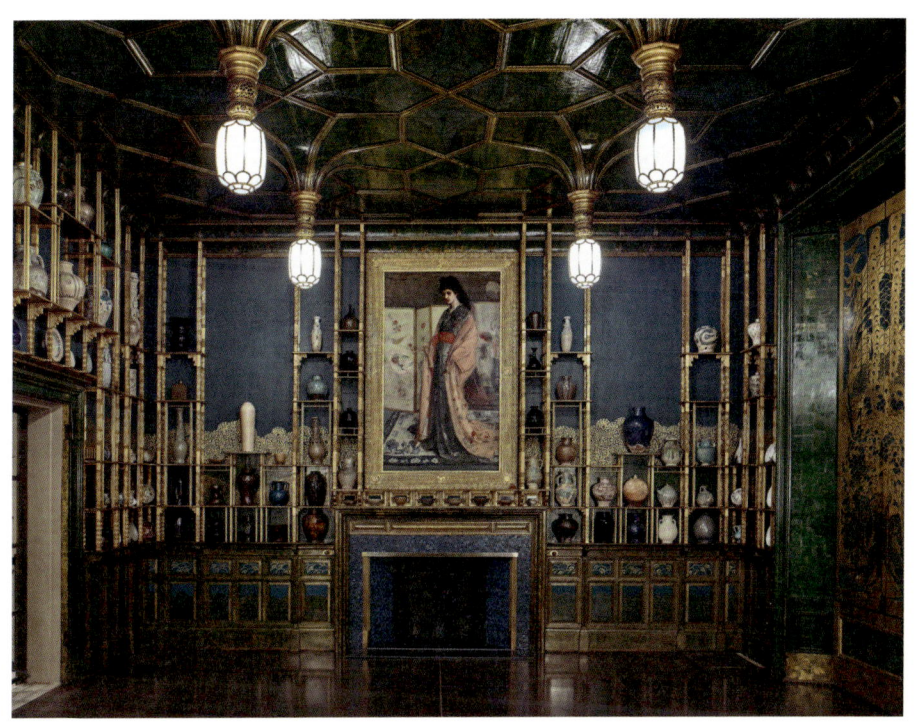

walls pink-grey, covered the floors in yellow matting, installed maroon couches, and spaciously hung his works, punctuated with plants, flowers and vases. He would go on to give titles to his exhibitions which similarly emphasised their cohesion, such as 1884's *Arrangement in Flesh Colour & Grey*, his instructions for which extended to the clothing worn by gallery attendants. In time he also sought to implement his ideas more widely, particularly after he became President of the Society of British Artists (SBA), an alternative exhibiting society to the Royal Academy, in 1886. There, in the manner of his own exhibitions, he began installing works more sparsely, and sought to arrange them in a unified way. Another of his innovations was the 'velarium', a ceiling-mounted drapery he designed to direct the sunlight entering the gallery, which can be seen in sketches he made of SBA exhibitions (p.73).

Harmony in Blue and Gold: The Peacock Room 1876–7
Oil paint and gold leaf on leather and wood
425 × 1010 × 608

Whistler also expressed his display ideas through the interior design projects he devised for patrons, most famously *Harmony in Blue and Gold: The Peacock Room* for Leyland (above). Whistler initially advised Leyland on a colour scheme to

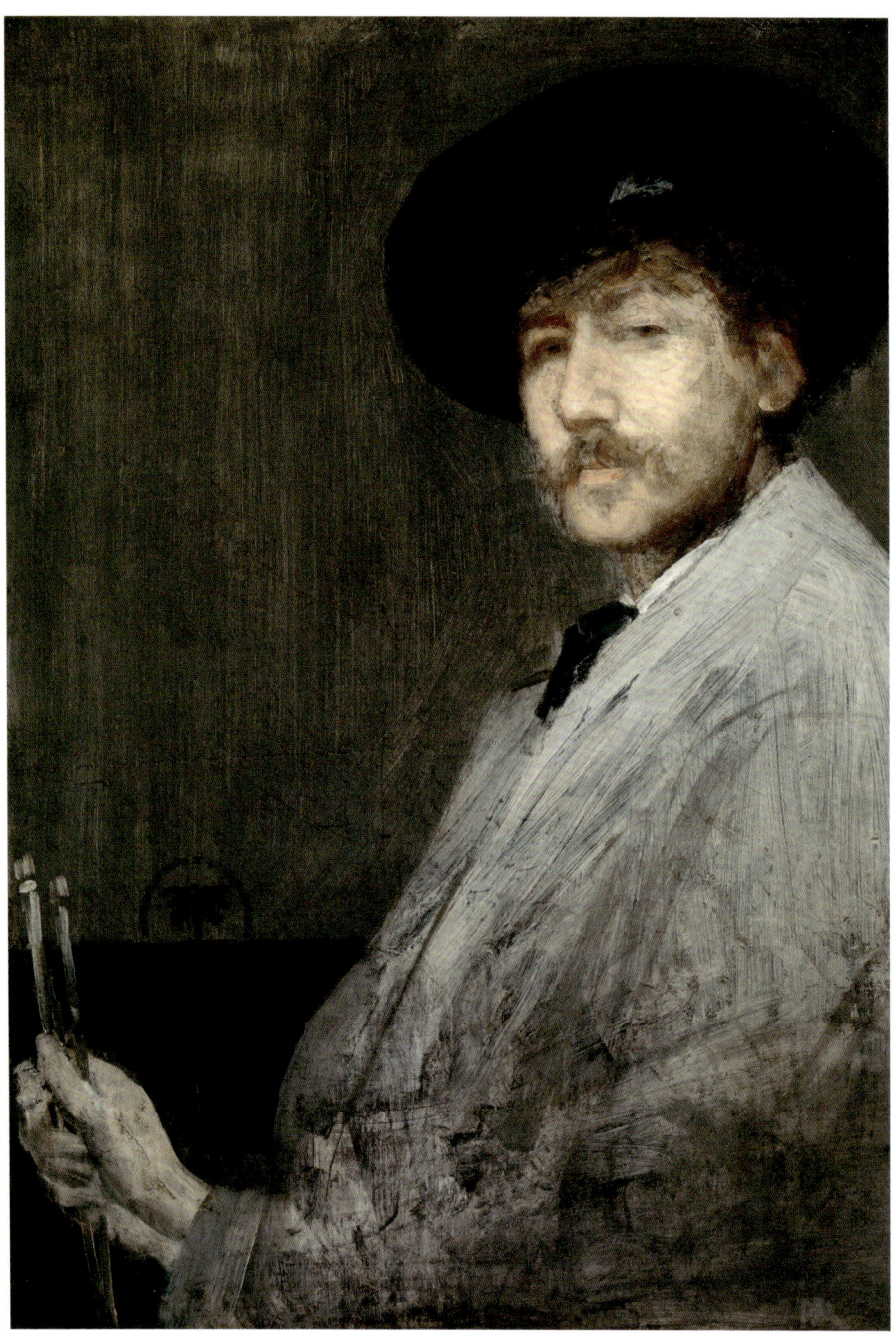

complement the artist's own *La Princesse du Pays de la Porcelaine*
1863–5 (p.43), which hung in the shipowner's London dining
room – a room specially adapted by Thomas Jeckyll for its
display. Whistler, however, took full advantage of the
opportunity to decorate the entire room. The entire dining
room was later purchased by another patron, Charles Freer,
and transported to the United States where it remains on
display at the Freer Gallery of Art in Washington, DC.

THE POLEMICIST

The tranquillity of Whistler's paintings was in stark contrast
to his combative personality. Throughout his career, Whistler
seldom let any perceived slight against him – or the artistic
principles he held dear – pass without retaliation, an attitude
of defiance captured in his 1872 self-portrait (opposite). This
brought him into conflict with several formidable figures.
In 1876, for instance, he severed ties with Leyland, then his
most important patron, following a dispute over payment for
the Peacock Room: Whistler requested a fee of 2,000 guineas,
but Leyland paid less than half of that, reflecting the disparity
between the commission and the work Whistler went on to
do.[23] Whistler incorporated the feud into the decoration of the
room itself, his panel 'The Rich Peacock and the Poor Peacock'
representing Leyland and Whistler respectively. The following
year, Whistler brought libel charges against Britain's most
celebrated critic, John Ruskin. After visiting an exhibition
of Whistler's work, Ruskin wrote with particular reference to
Nocturne in Black and Gold: The Falling Rocket 1875 (p.57): 'I have
seen, and heard, much of Cockney impudence before now;
but never expected to hear a coxcomb ask two hundred guineas
for flinging a pot of paint in the public's face.'[24] The painting
was in fact meticulously executed, but Ruskin, who valued
truthfulness in art above all else, was troubled by what he saw
as conduct approaching 'wilful imposture' on Whistler's part.[25]
An outraged Whistler seized the opportunity to defend his
artistic principles, and took centre stage in the eventual trial.
Choice exchanges were published in the newspapers, elevating
the trial to a major public event (Whistler also published a
pamphlet recounting the trial, *Whistler v. Ruskin: Art & Art Critics*).

The outcome was a pyrrhic victory for Whistler: the court
found in his favour but only awarded damages of one farthing,
with both parties instructed to pay their legal costs. This
posed serious difficulties for Whistler, who had recently

commissioned the architect E.W. Godwin to build a radical home-studio for him on Tite Street, the 'White House' (since demolished). Amid mounting financial difficulties, Whistler declared bankruptcy in 1879, losing, in the process, the White House (bought by another enemy, the critic Harry Quilter) together with his art and his porcelain collection.

This experience did nothing to chasten Whistler, who continued to rail against his critics. In the mould of celebrity speakers such as Charles Dickens and Oscar Wilde, Whistler devised a lecture, the '10 O'Clock' (referring to the unusually late starting time), delivered in 1885 and also published in pamphlet form. Taking aim at his frenemy Wilde and other doubters, the '10 O'Clock' was a masterful defence of Whistler's 'art for art's sake' ideals, and an elegant rebuttal of claims to art's social or political imperatives. The lecture resonated with the French symbolist poet Stéphane Mallarmé, who translated it into French and became a close friend of Whistler's (p.81). When Whistler published a collection of his pugnacious correspondence in 1892 he titled it, with typical suavity, The Gentle Art of Making Enemies.

VENICE

Financial peril in the wake of the Ruskin trial prompted Whistler's return to printmaking as a more reliable source of income than his paintings. In 1879 the Fine Art Society, who had recently purchased many of Whistler's earlier plates in order to publish new editions, commissioned him to make twelve etchings of Venice, a commission that also offered Whistler a convenient way to absent himself from London.

Whistler and his partner of the time Maud Franklin left for Venice in September 1879. Their stay began badly: the winter of 1879, he wrote, was 'woefully cold ... the bitterest winter I fancy I ever experienced', making it difficult for him to work.[26] The result, however, was a creative flourishing, as a result of which Whistler did not return to London until November 1880. He etched fifty plates in Venice (most of which were published in two sets) and made several paintings, together with more than a hundred drawings in pastel, constituting his major body of work in that medium (pp.66–7). Whistler used pastels straight from the box, making little attempt to alter or enrich the colour, and deployed the brown of his chosen paper as a colour in itself. Unlike Edgar Degas, who developed complicated techniques to make his pastels

Nocturne: Palaces 1879–80
Etching and drypoint on paper
29.8 × 20.2

18

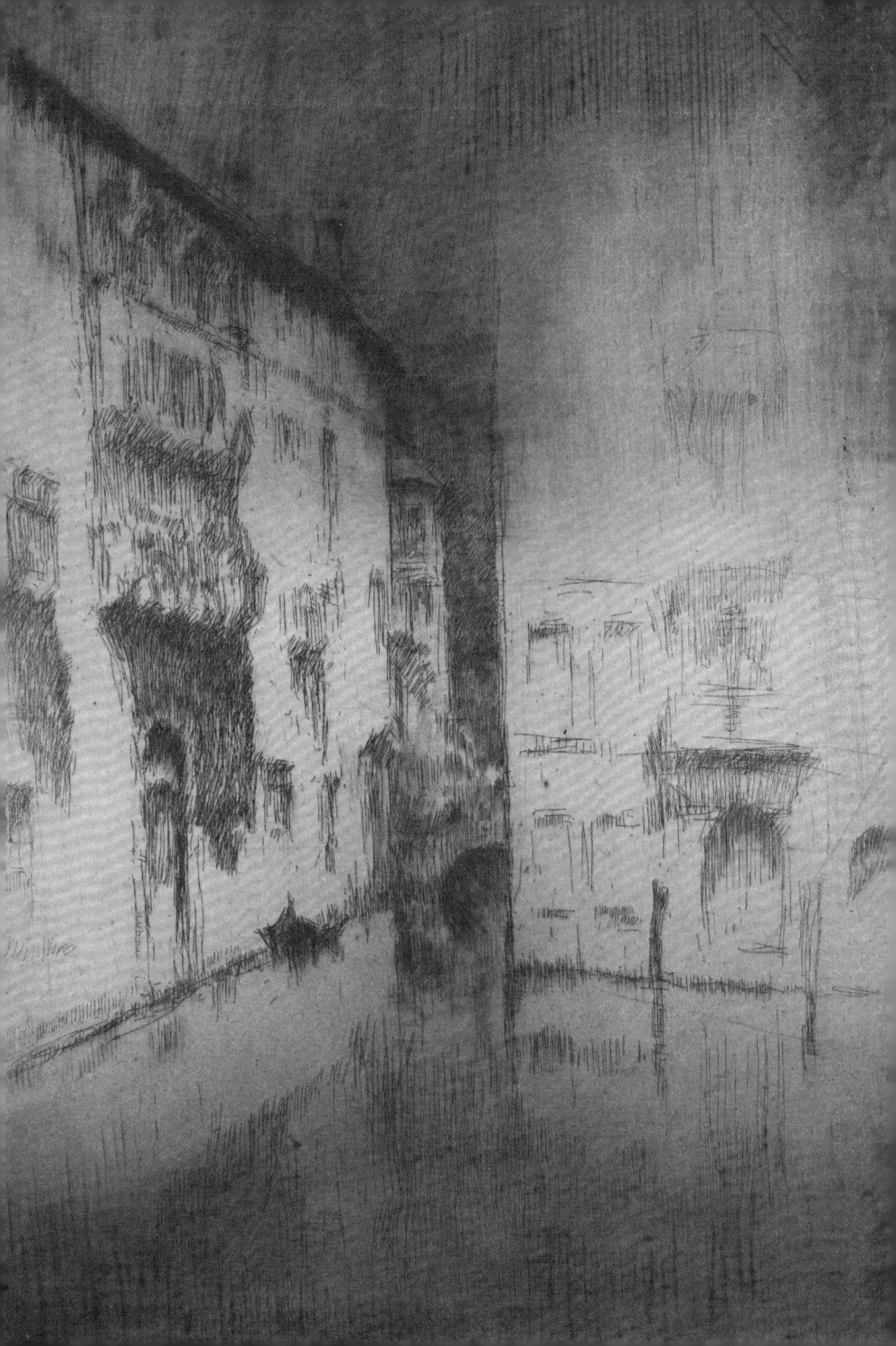

seem more like oil paintings, Whistler relished the distinct properties of the medium.[27]

'I have learned to know a Venice within Venice that the others seem never to have perceived', Whistler triumphantly declared.[28] As with his Thames etchings and nocturnes, Whistler was able to find new ways of depicting a city that many artists had tackled before him, exploring Venice's quiet corners and capturing its mysterious poetry. Some of the most distinctive prints adopt extremes of perspective: in *The Little Venice* 1880 (p.65) a panoramic view of the city from the Lido is concentrated into a narrow horizontal band, with expanses of water below and sky above rendered only in the subtlest detail. *Nocturne: Palaces* 1879–80 (p.19), meanwhile, records in intricate detail the facades of Venetian buildings. In his Venetian project Whistler also reconfigured his approach to printmaking, asserting control over all aspects of production and display (aided by trusted assistants such as Walter Sickert). Where he had previously worked with a professional printer, Whistler now insisted on overseeing the printing of each impression himself, making numerous revisions (one print, *Fruit Stall*, from the 'Second Venice Set', ran to twenty-one distinct states). He also used techniques such as adding ink washes to the plate (known as plate-tone) before pulling each impression of etchings such as *Nocturne: Palaces*. As a result, each impression of these prints is fundamentally unique. The French artist Camille Pissarro, himself a skilled printmaker, noted that the distinctive shimmer produced by the plate-tone technique could be attributed to the artist's direct involvement, and that 'no professional printer could replace him'.[29] This may explain why Whistler still had not finished printing the edition of the 'First Venice Set' agreed with the Fine Art Society at the time of his death, over twenty years after the plates were etched (the edition was completed posthumously). In his Venice prints Whistler introduced what became the standard presentation of his etchings, trimming them to the platemark and around a tab on the lower margin, which he signed with his butterfly monogram and the abbreviation 'imp.' to indicate that he had printed it himself. This helped to establish the now standard practice of artists signing their prints individually.

Whistler considered the culmination of his work as a printmaker to be a series of prints he made in Amsterdam in 1889. Appraising his graphic work in three stages (the first represented by the Thames Set, the second by his Venice prints), he described his Amsterdam prints, which again focused on the city's buildings and canals, as combining 'the elaboration of the first stage, and the quality of the second'.[30] It was these prints that the playwright George Bernard Shaw described as 'the most exquisite renderings by the most independent man of the century' (p.76).[31]

PORTRAITS

Demand for a portrait by Whistler fluctuated with the artist's reputation. In the 1870s he attracted not only wealthy businessmen but also celebrities such as the renowned historian Thomas Carlyle and the actor Sir Henry Irving who consented to being painted as 'arrangements' of colour and design. He was slyly alive to portraiture's capacity for performance and artifice – Irving was depicted as Philip II of Spain, the same year as he played the role in Alfred, Lord Tennyson's verse play *Queen Mary Tudor*, while Maud Franklin was painted as Effie Deans, a character from Walter Scott's 1818 novel *The Heart of Mid-Lothian* (pp.58–9).

After Whistler's bankruptcy in 1879 he lost access to the conservative patrons he had painted in the previous decade, such as the Leyland and Alexander families. Whistler's portrait subjects of the following decade tended to be either those who belonged to the same avant-garde circles – among them the critics and collectors Théodore Duret (p.69) and Comte Robert de Montesquiou-Fezensac (p.80) – or those willing to flout convention, such as Lady Meux (p.62). In 1888, Whistler married the artist Beatrice Godwin, the widow of E.W. Godwin (architect of the White House), who he had painted in another celebrated portrait of this period, *Harmony in Red: Lamplight* 1884–6 (p.22). Whistler's later portraits became increasingly austere. He stripped away anything extraneous, perfecting a format in which his sitter stood full-length, isolated against a dark background.

Success in the 1890s brought a resurgence of high-profile commissions from the likes of George W. Vanderbilt, a fabulously wealthy American collector, although Whistler's prevarications meant there was never any danger of him becoming a prolific painter of commissioned portraits in the manner of his Chelsea neighbour John Singer Sargent: the Vanderbilt portrait remained unfinished at the time of Whistler's death, six years after he had started it. Whistler's favoured models remained

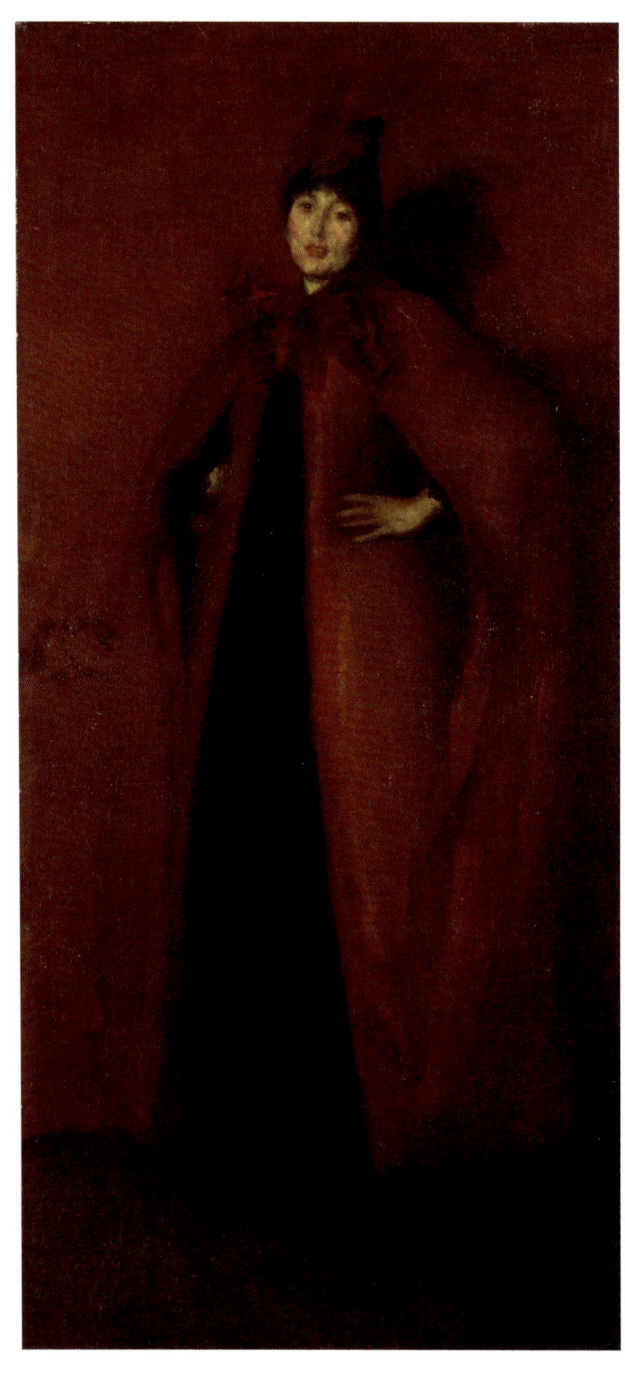

Harmony in Red:
Lamplight 1884–6
Oil paint on canvas
190.5 × 89.7

those with whom he was closest – his sister-in-law Ethel Philip, for instance (p.87). And then there was the one sitter who could always be relied upon to understand the artist's intentions – Whistler himself (p.91).

FINAL YEARS

In the 1890s Whistler's works began to enter major public collections. Having refused to part with it for many years, Whistler sold *Portrait of the Painter's Mother* to the Musée du Luxembourg, Paris in 1891 (a sale facilitated by Mallarmé and Duret), granting him the French state recognition he had long coveted.[32] The city of Glasgow purchased the portrait of Carlyle that same year, while in 1892 a triumphant retrospective exhibition at the Goupil Gallery in London was met with widespread acclaim. A succession of international honours and accolades came Whistler's way in his final decade.

Whistler and Beatrice moved to Paris in 1892, where she encouraged his use of lithography, another form of printmaking in which Whistler became prolific. The finest of his lithographs, such as the earlier *Nocturne* 1878 (made from memory in one sitting in the office of his printer Thomas Way) incorporated washes evoking the liquid textures of his paintings (p.64). After Beatrice developed cancer in 1894, however, the couple returned to England for treatment. In Lyme Regis Whistler made exquisite portraits of people he met there (pp.84–5), and in 1896, staying at the Savoy Hotel during Beatrice's final weeks, Whistler produced his last lithographs of her and the view of the Thames from their balcony (pp.88–9). They contain a poignancy unmatched in his work.

Whistler was devastated by Beatrice's death but continued to pursue new projects. From 1898 he taught at the Paris atelier of his former model Carmen Rossi, where he taught pupils including Gwen John, and he established the Company of the Butterfly as a way of bypassing gallerists and selling directly to buyers. He also continued to travel regularly, including a trip taking in Marseille, Tangier, Algiers and Corsica (p.90).

Whistler died of heart failure in 1903. He was interred in Chiswick Cemetery, like his hero William Hogarth, whose work had inspired him since he was a child. In tribute, the critic Roger Fry wrote 'it was impossible to conceive of Mr. Whistler as an elderly man. He seemed to be always inaugurating a revolution, leading intransigent youth against the strongholds of tradition and academic complacence'.[33]

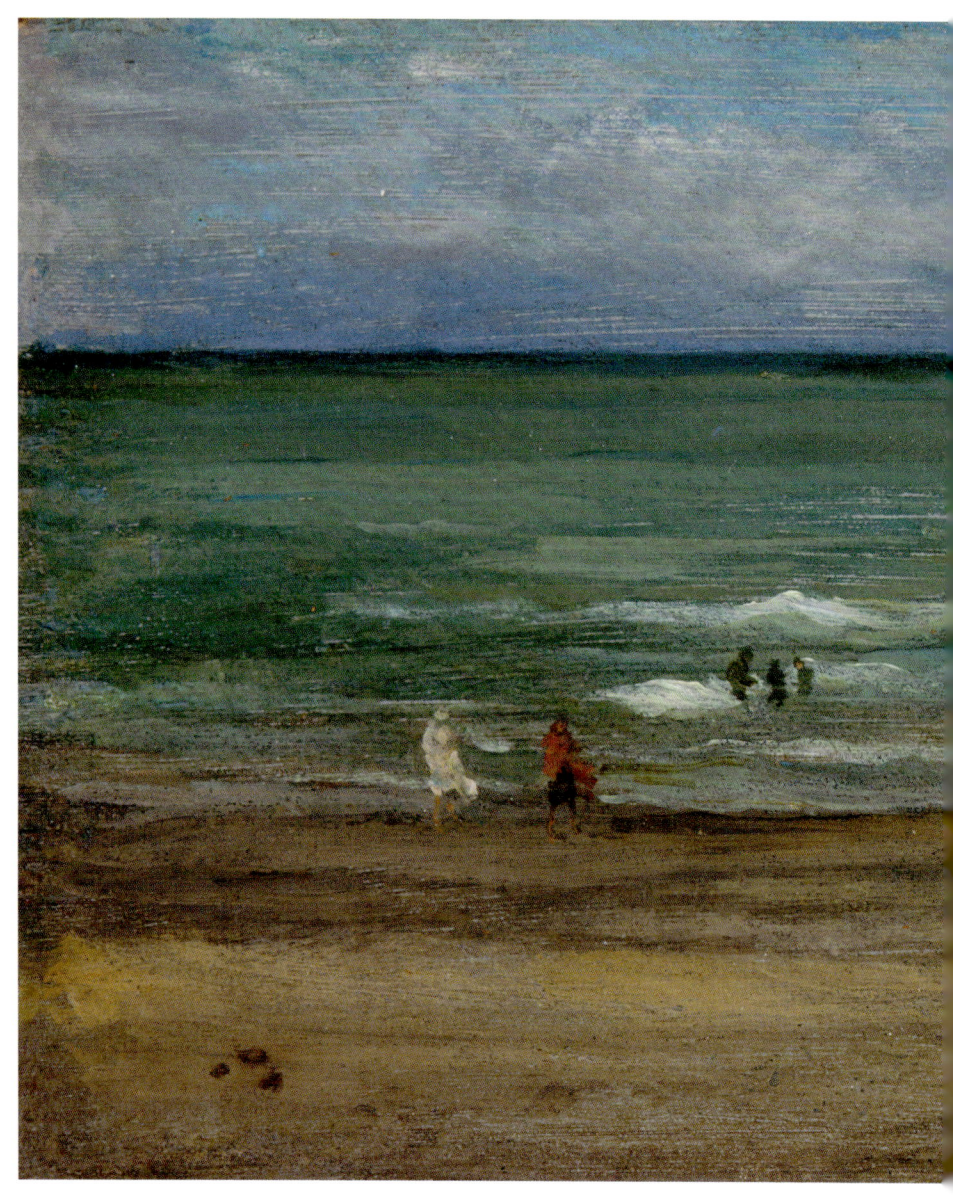

The Sea, Pourville 1899
Oil paint on wood
13.3 × 23.8

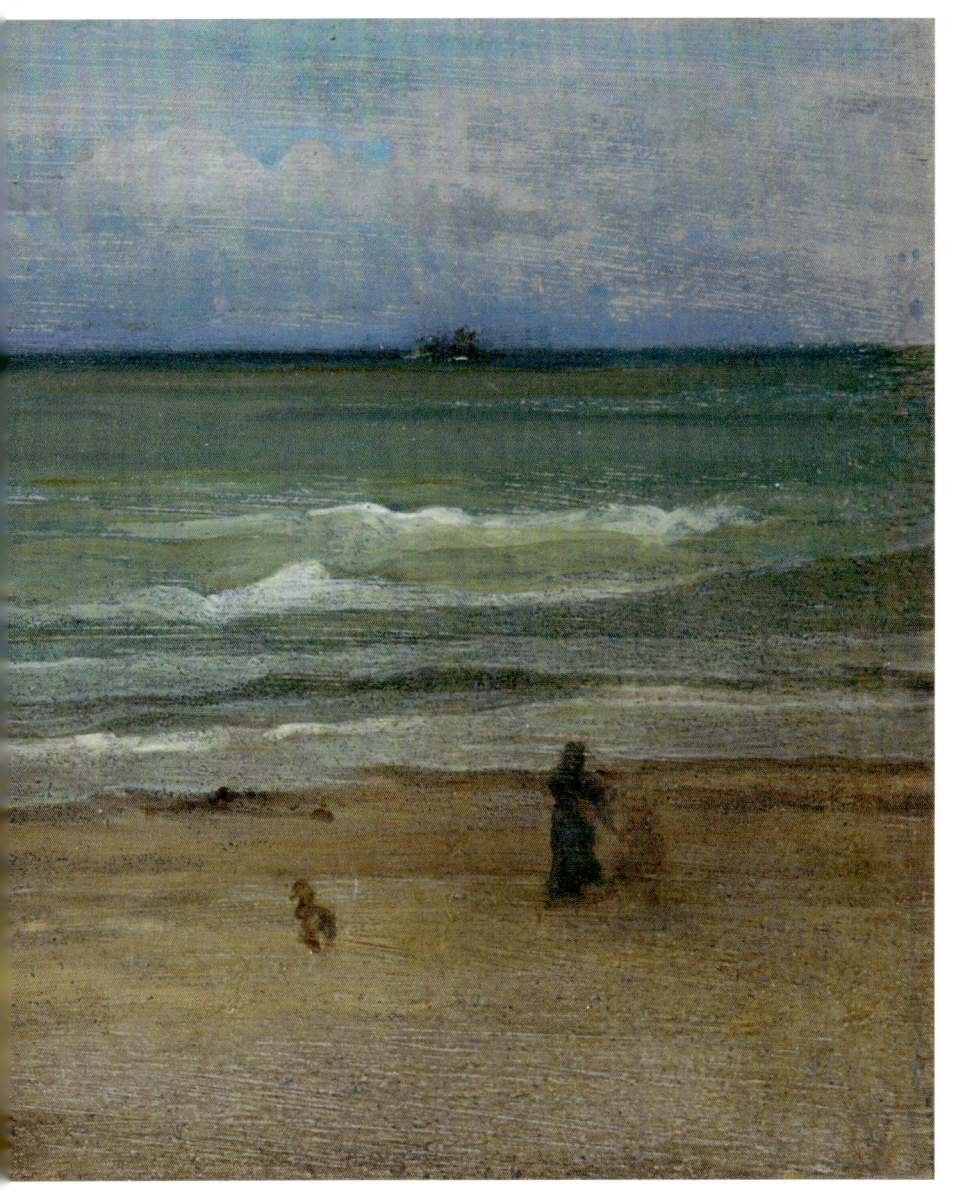

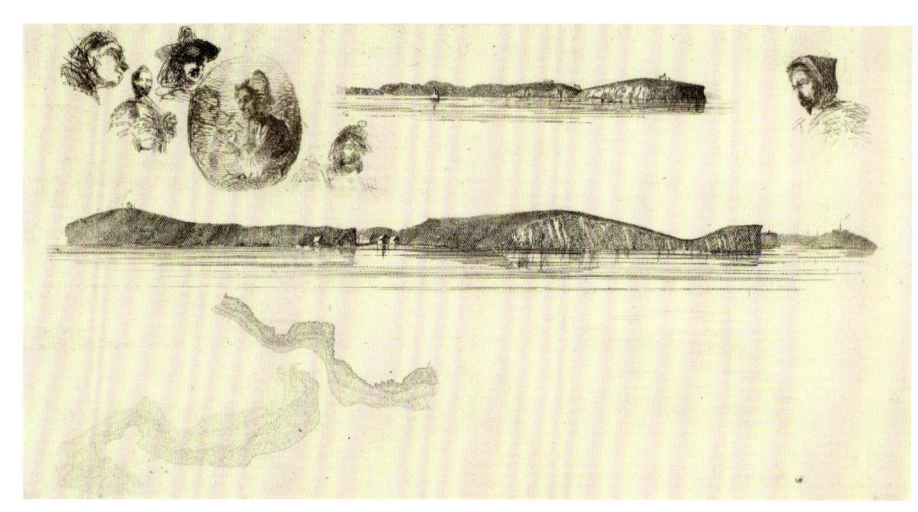

Sketches on the Coast Survey
Plate 1855
Etching on paper
14.9 × 25.3

La Mère Gérard 1858
Etching on paper
12.9 × 9

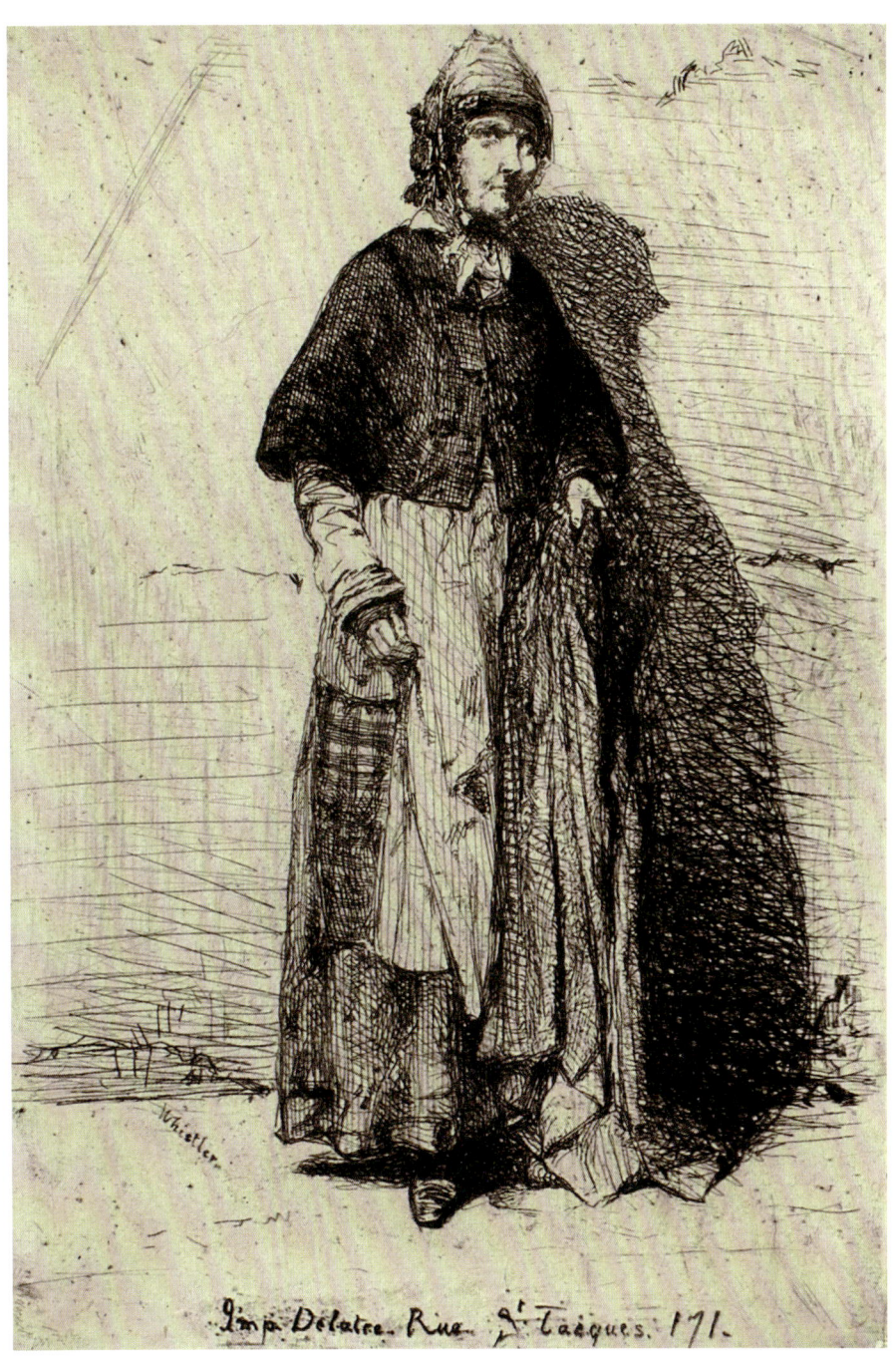

Imp. Delatre. Rue. St. Jacques. 171.

27

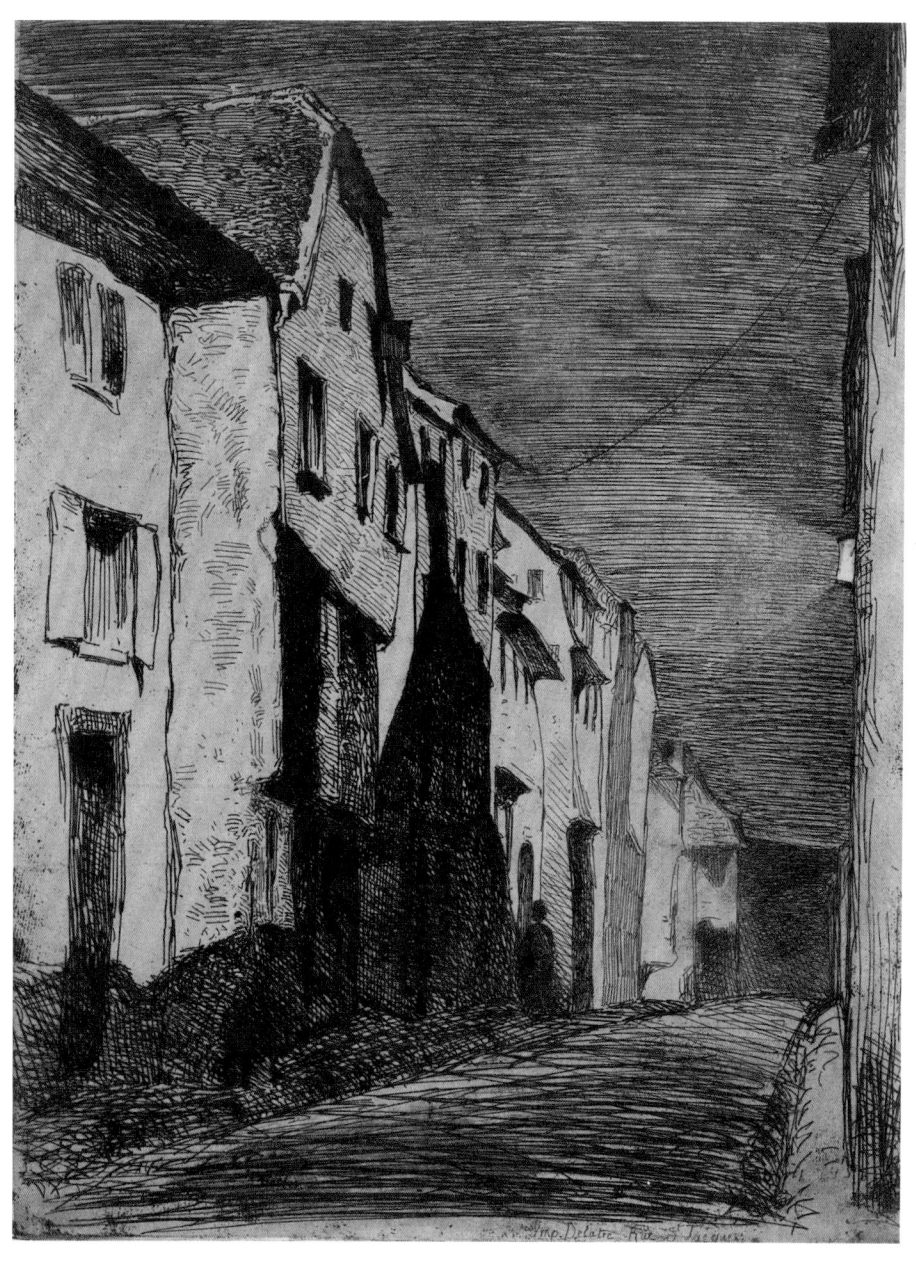

Street at Saverne 1858
Etching on paper
20.9 × 15.9

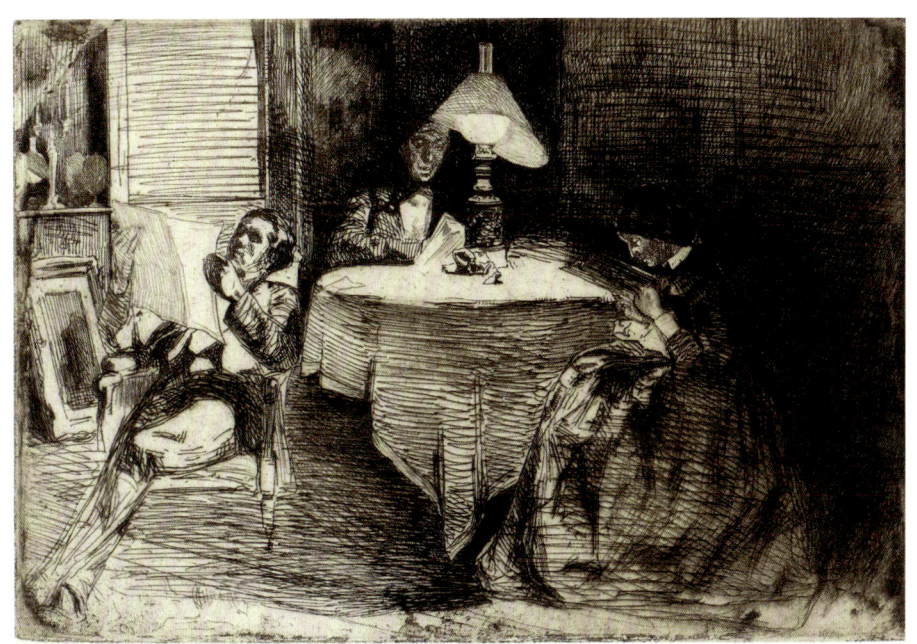

The Music Room 1859
Etching and drypoint
on paper
14.7 × 21.7

OVERLEAF
At the Piano 1858–9
Oil paint on canvas
67 × 90.5

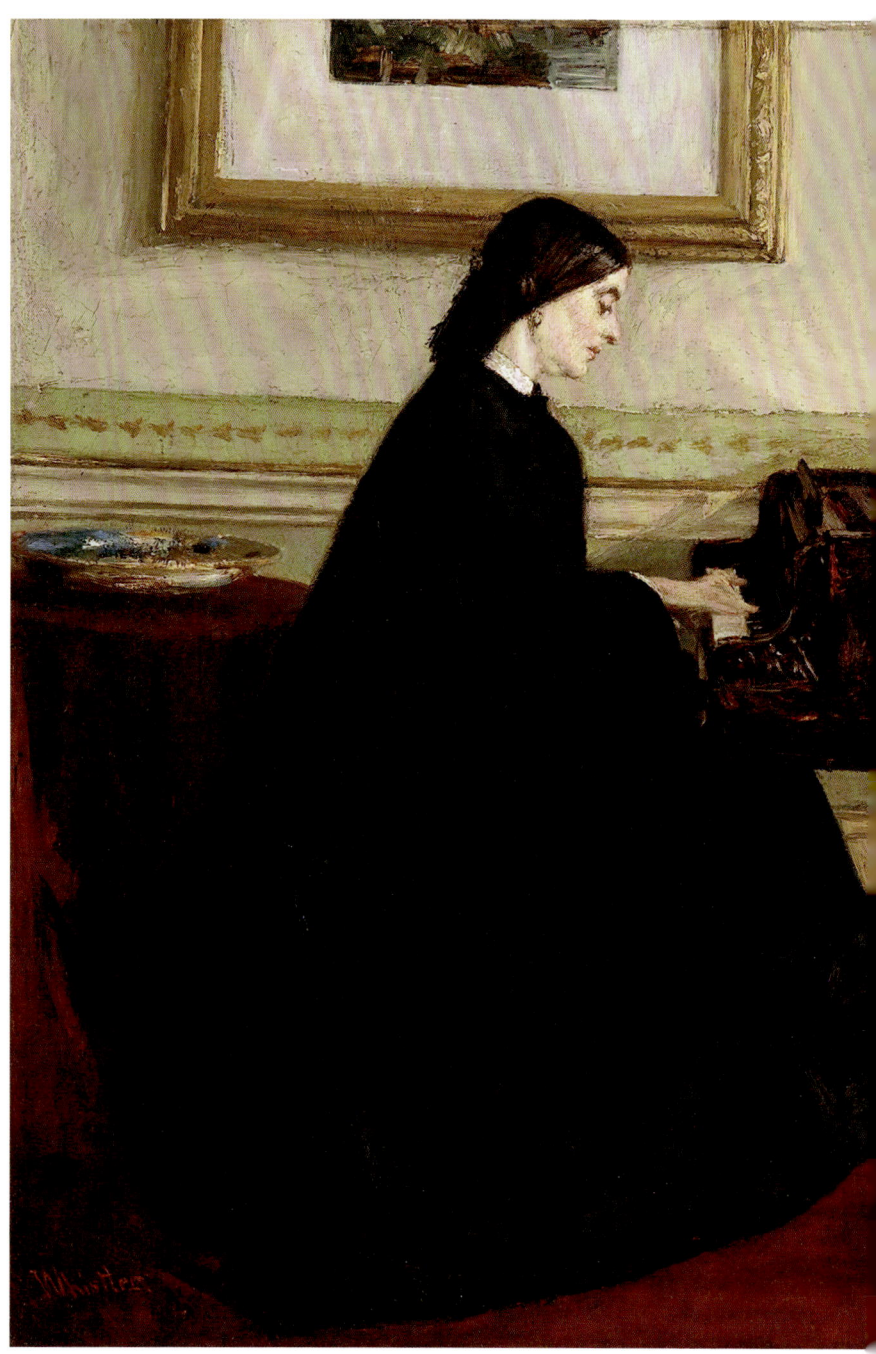

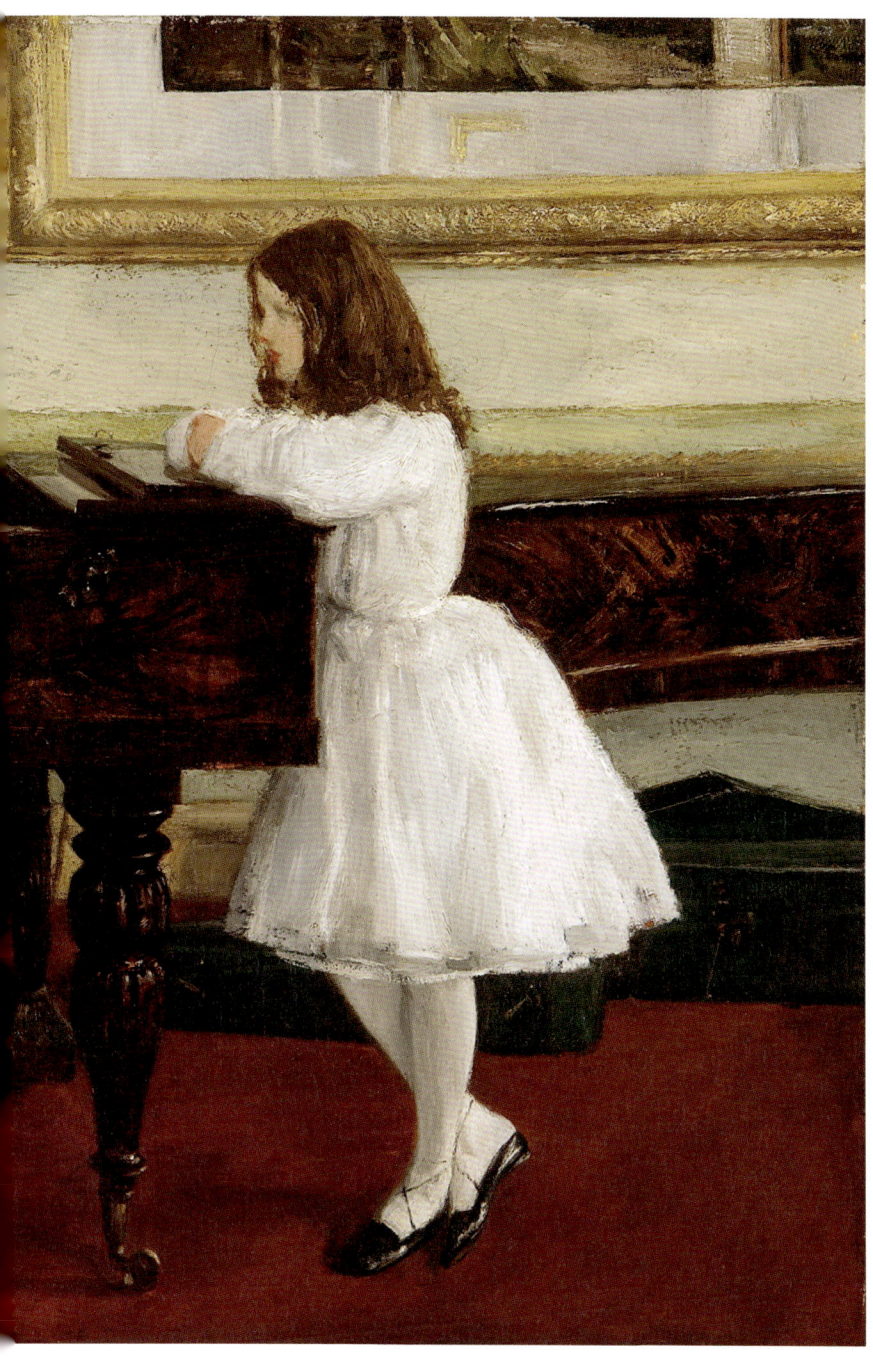

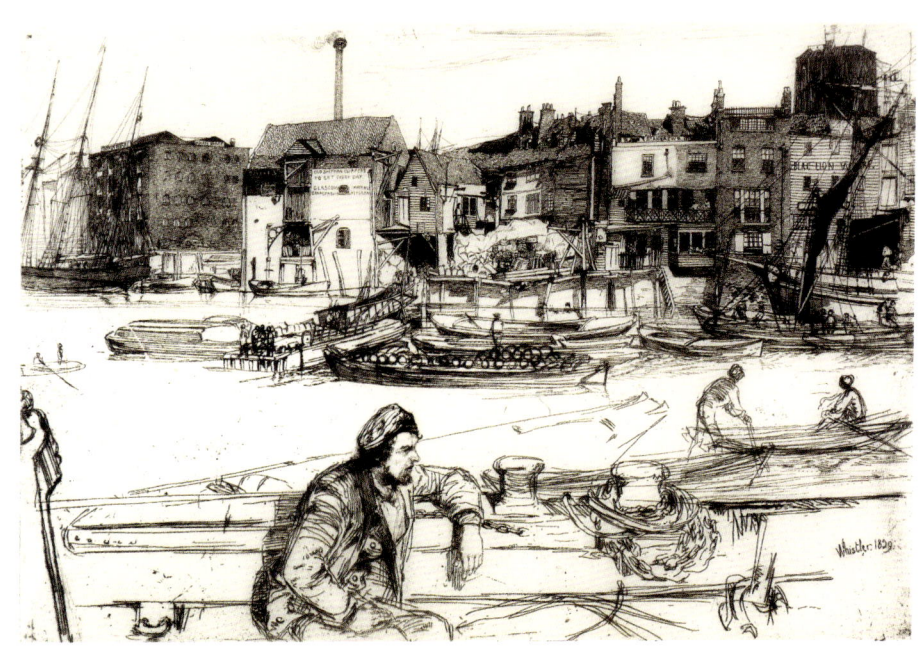

Black Lion Wharf 1859
Etching on paper
14.3 × 22.5

The Lime-Burner 1859
Etching and drypoint
on paper
25.5 × 17.9

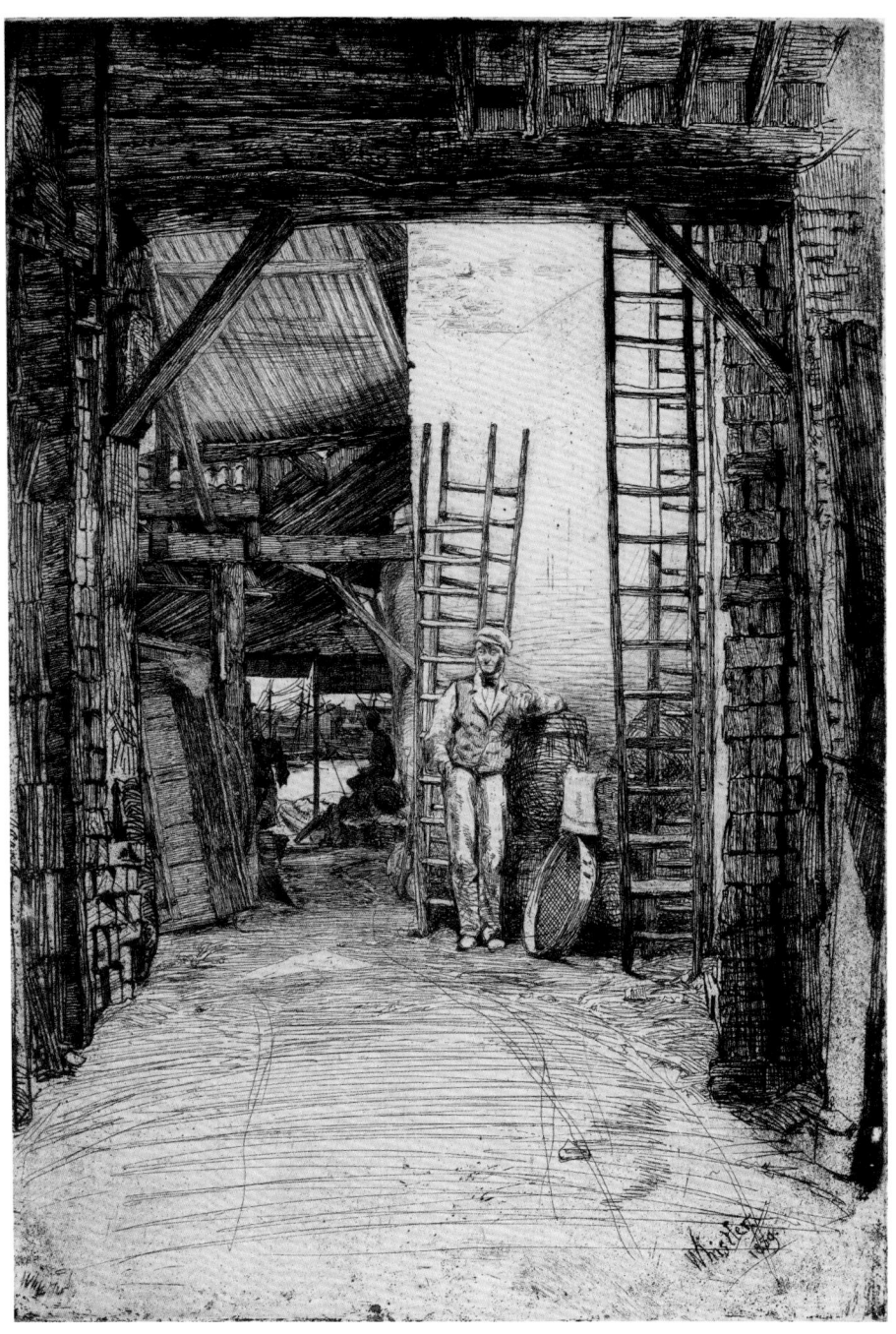

Brown and Silver: Old Battersea Bridge 1859–63
Oil paint on canvas
mounted on masonite
63.8 × 76

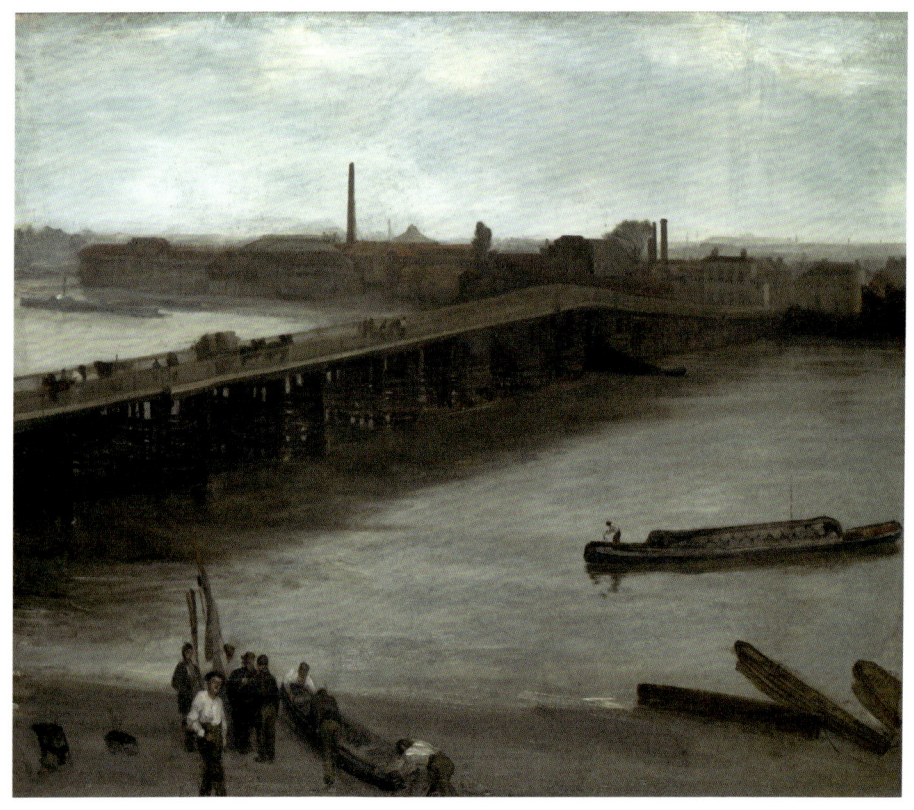

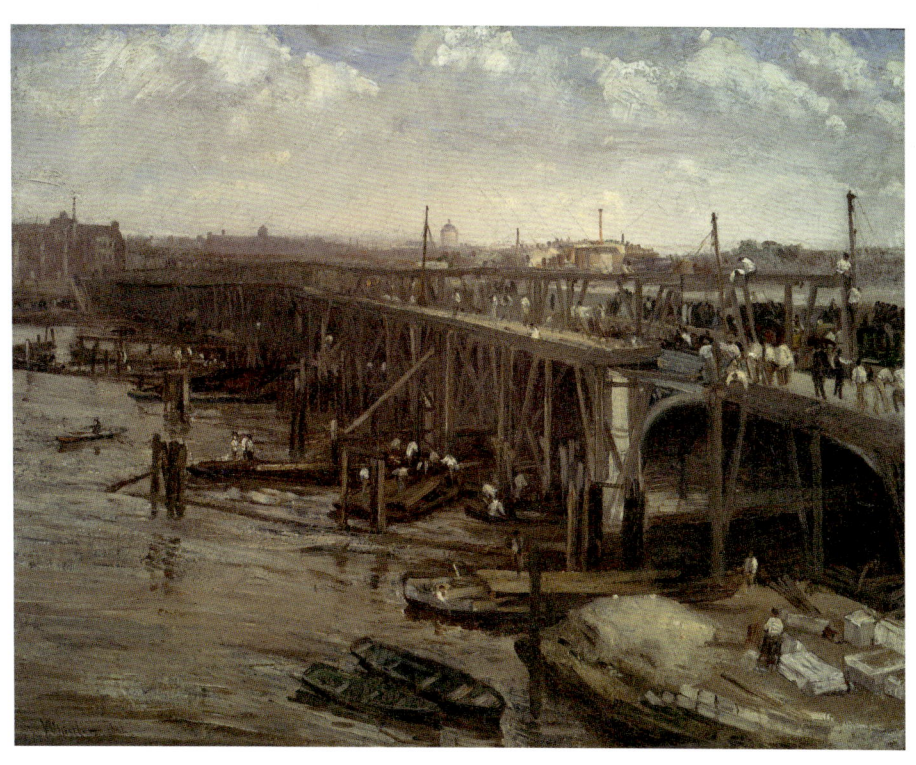

The Last of Old Westminster
1862
Oil paint on canvas
61 × 78.1

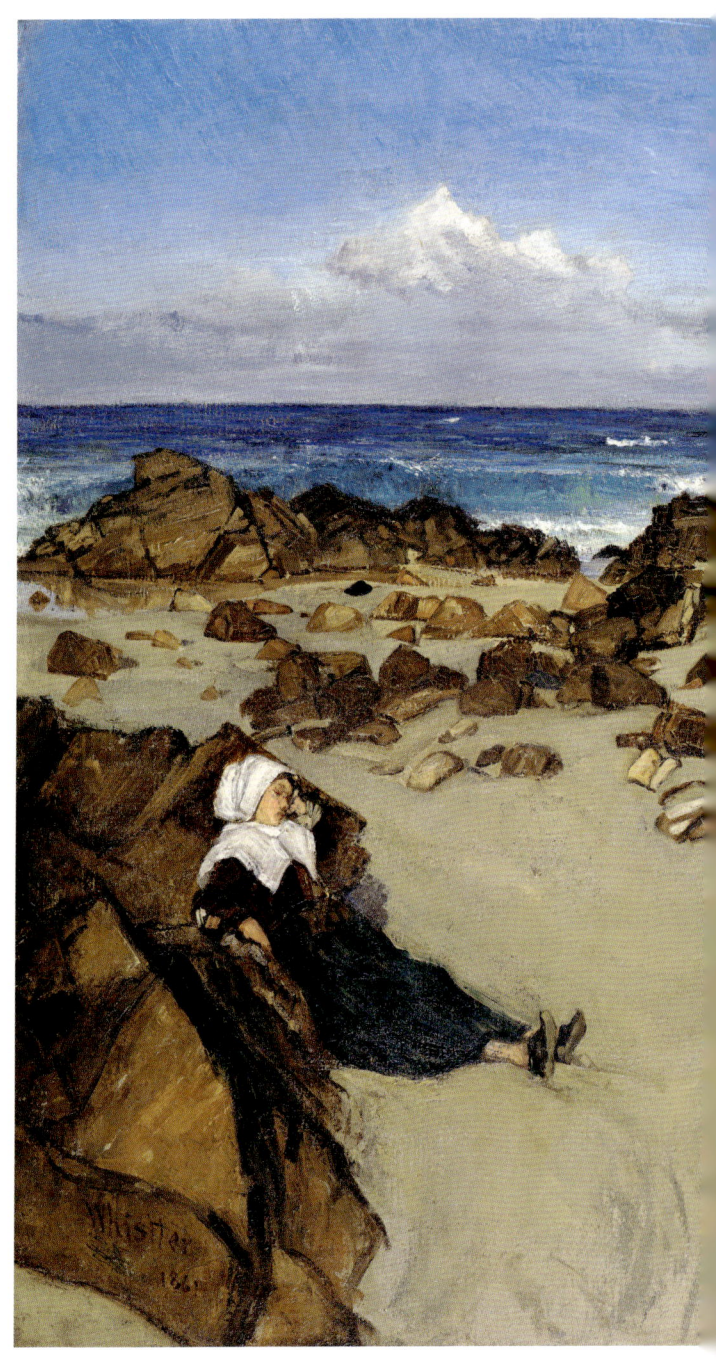

The Coast of Brittany 1861
Oil paint on canvas
87.3 × 115.6

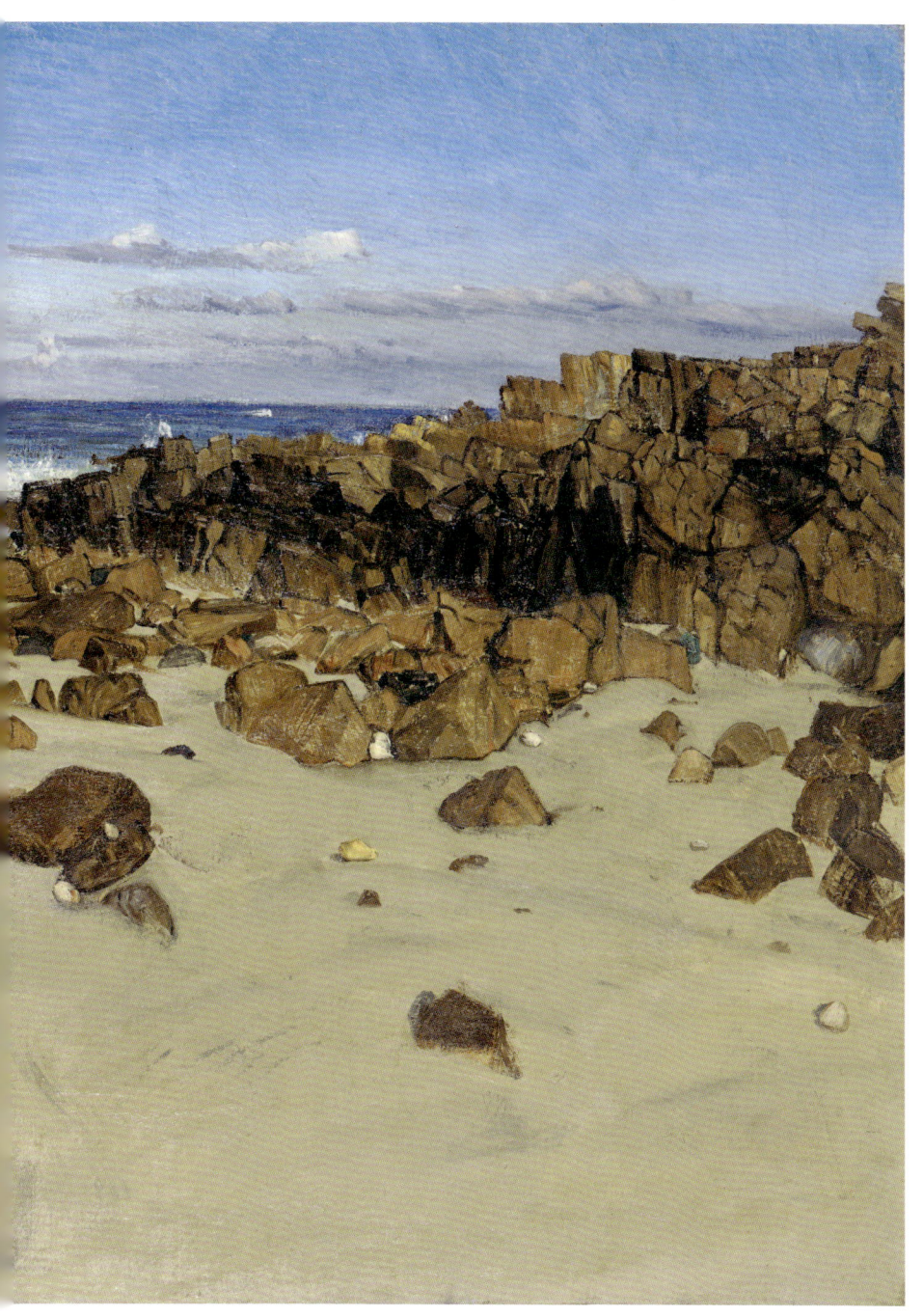

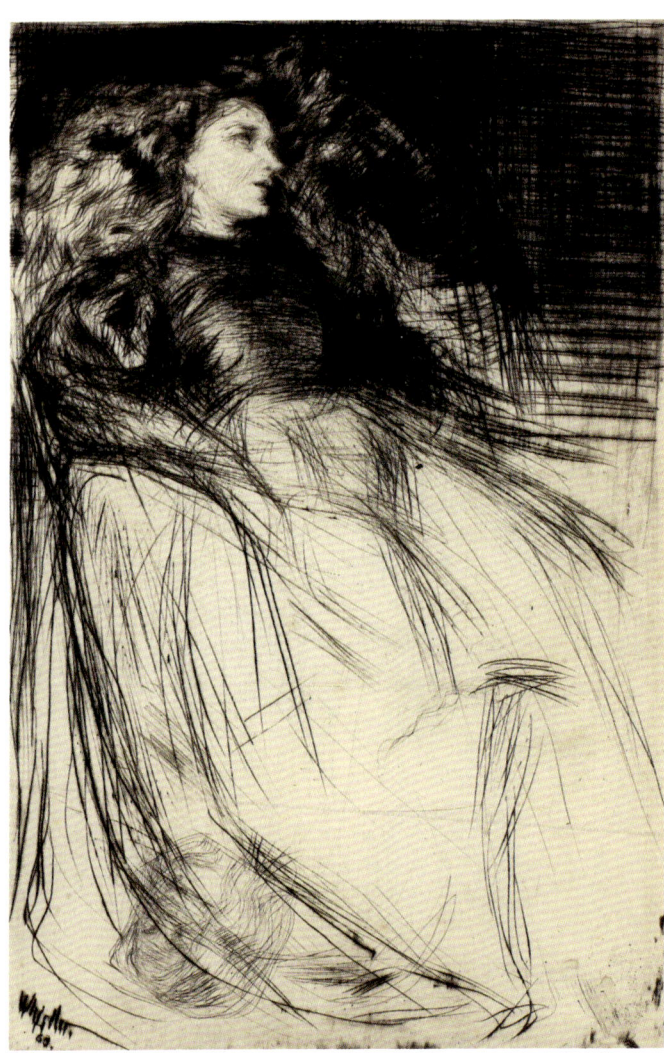

Weary 1863
Drypoint on paper
19.9 × 13.2

Symphony in White, No.2:
The Little White Girl 1864
Oil paint on canvas
76.5 × 51.1

OVERLEAF
Symphony in White, No.3
1865–7
Oil paint on canvas
52 × 76.5

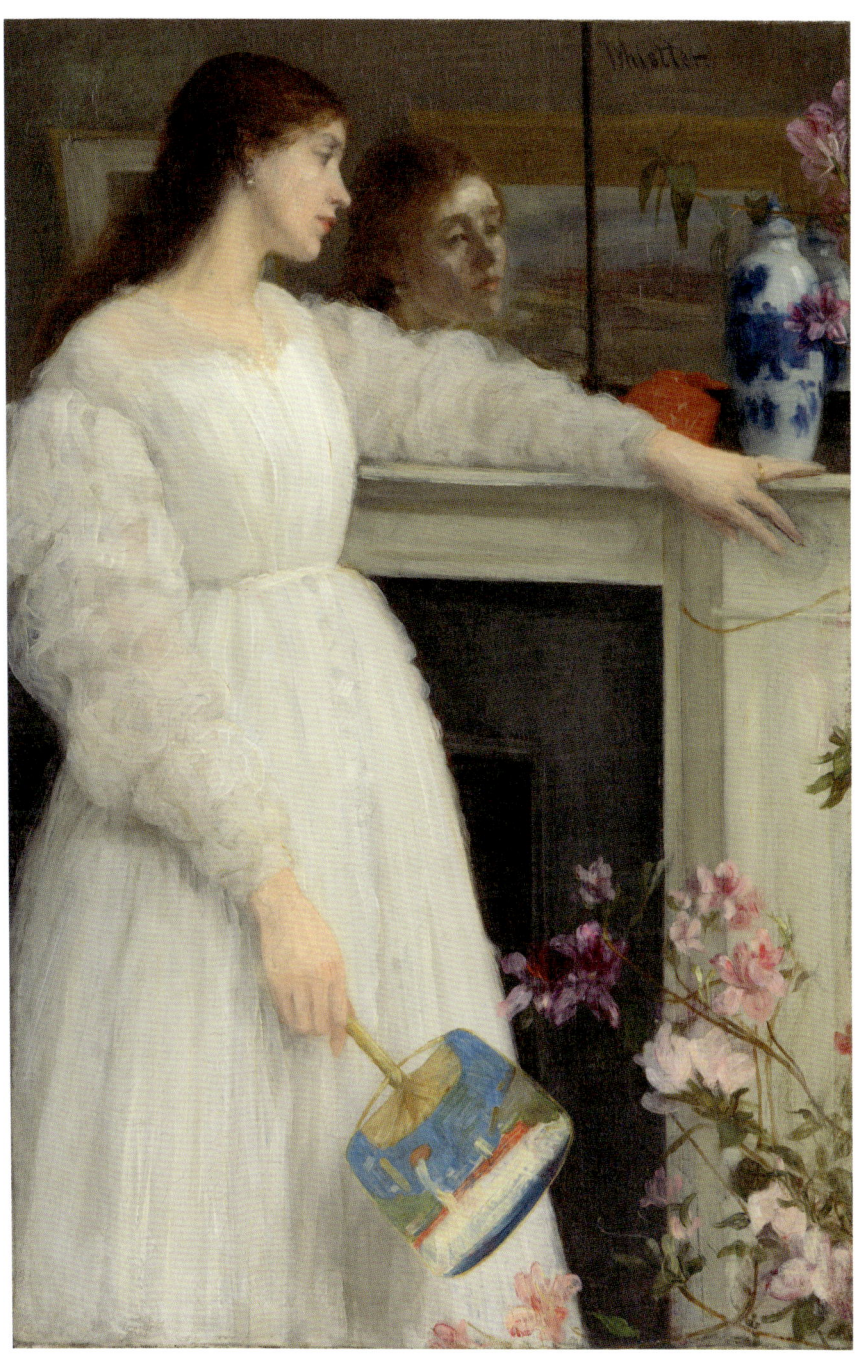

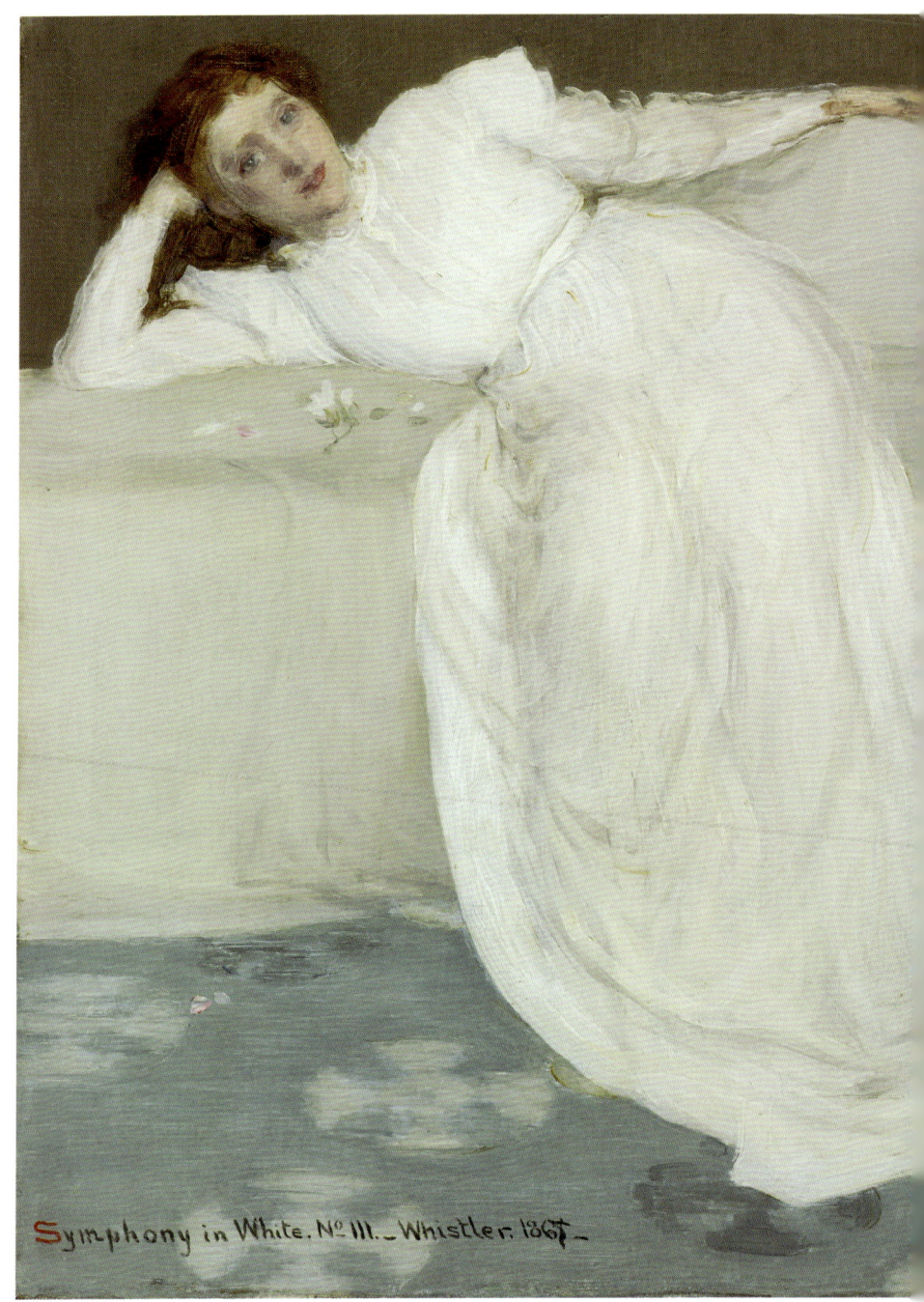

Symphony in White. No III. - Whistler. 1867 -

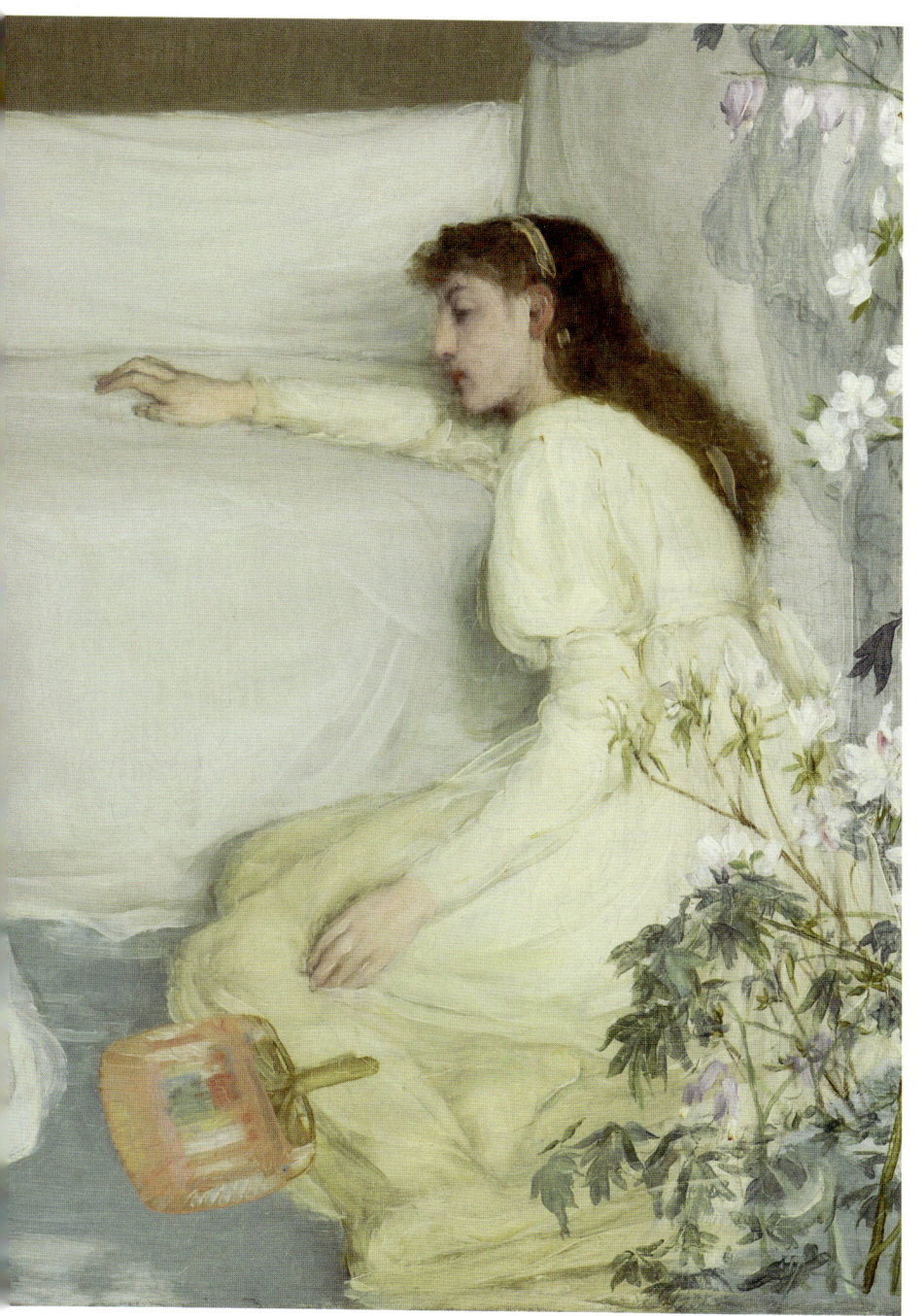

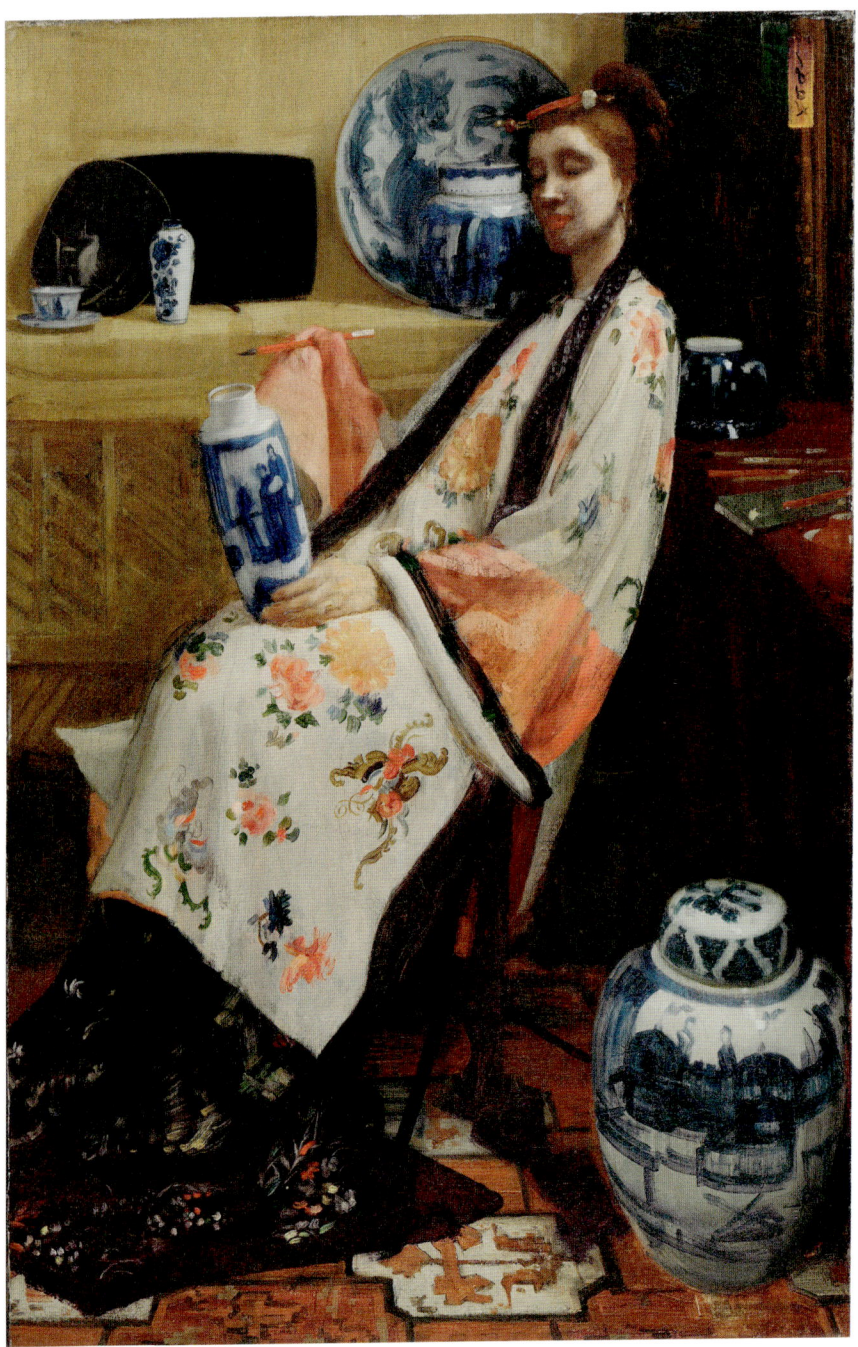

*Purple and Rose: The Lange
Leizen of the Six Marks* 1864
Oil paint on canvas
93.3 × 61.3

*La Princesse du Pays de la
Porcelaine* 1863–5
Oil paint on canvas
199.9 × 116

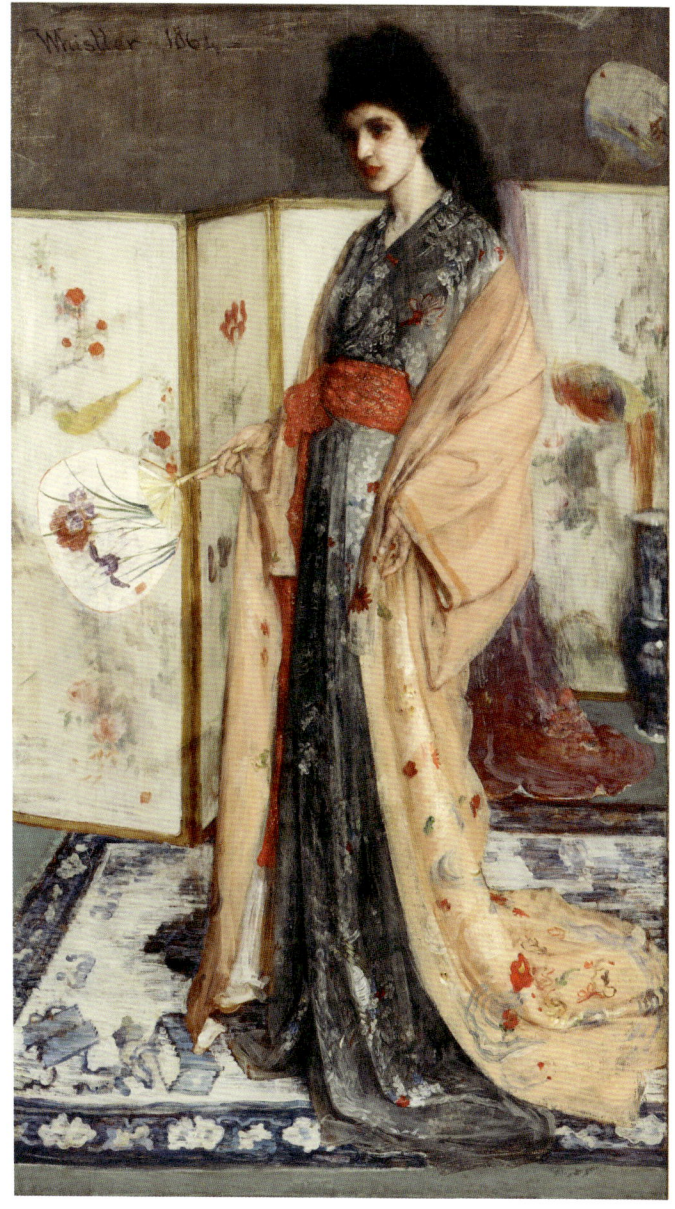

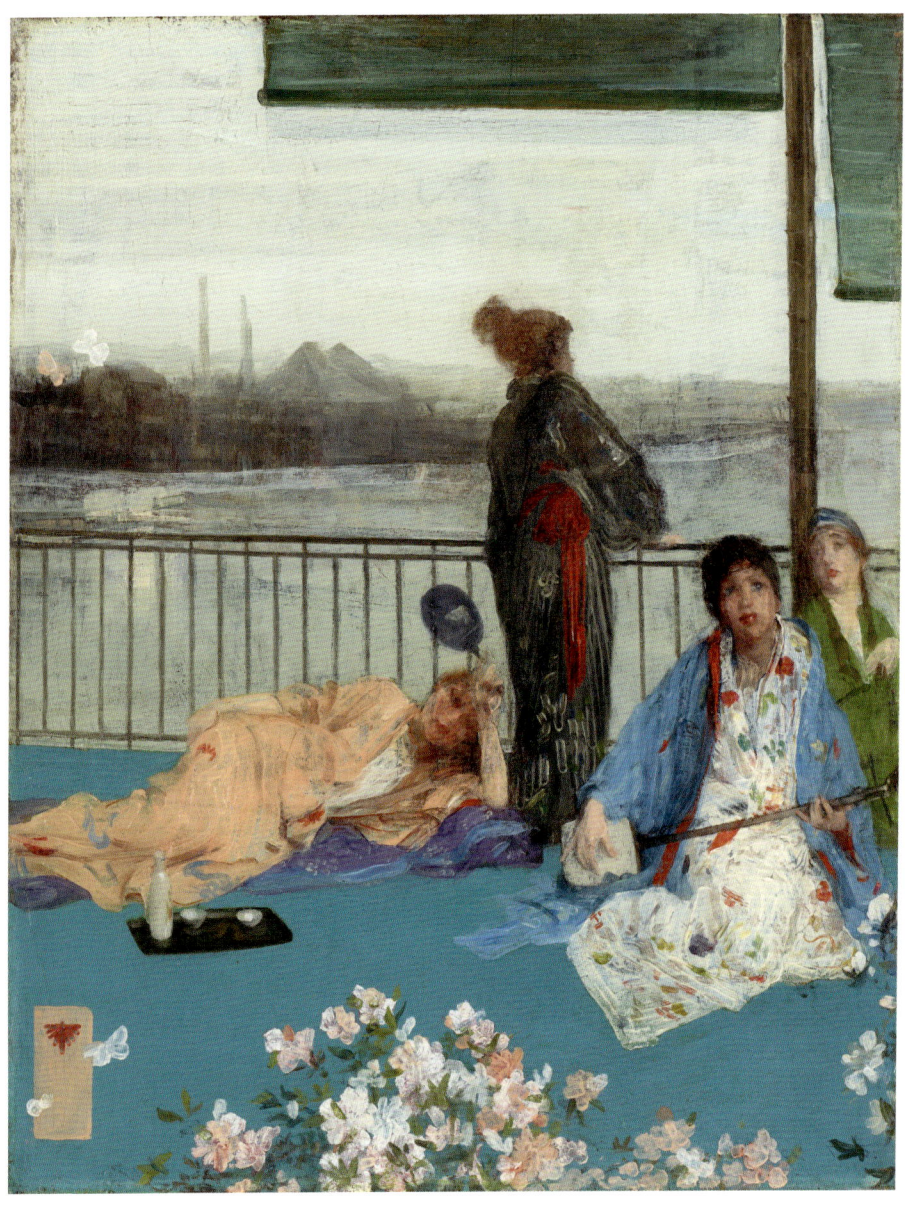

*Variations in Flesh Colour and
Green: The Balcony* 1864–73
Oil paint on wood
61.4 × 48.8

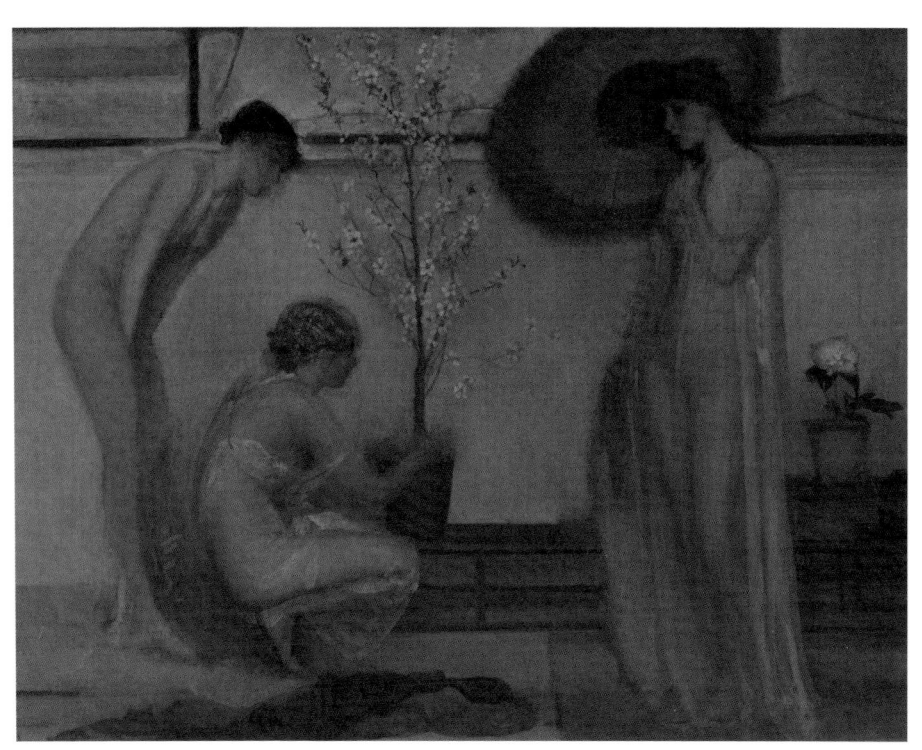

Three Figures: Pink and Grey
1868–78
Oil paint on canvas
139.1 × 185.4

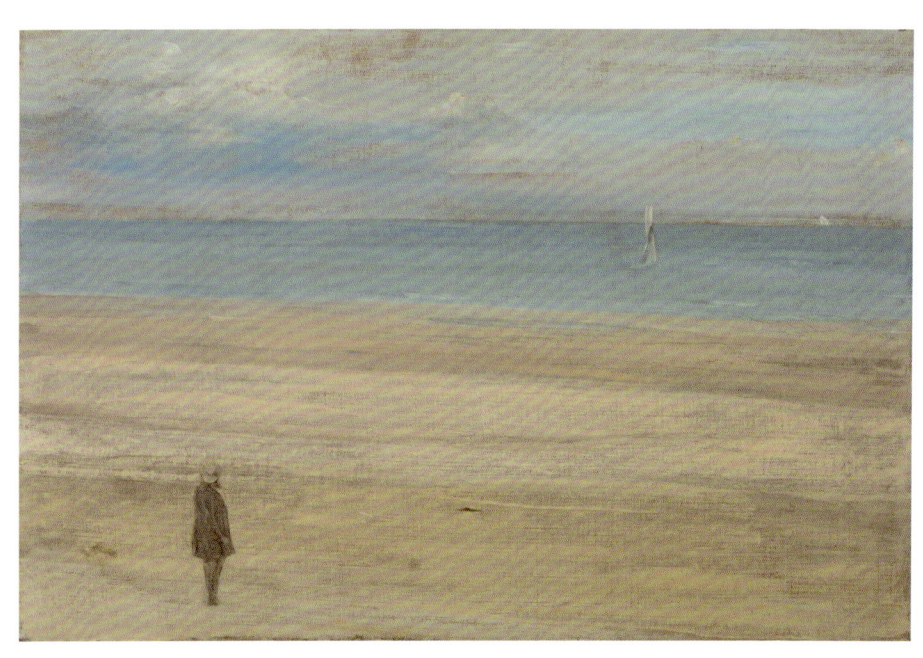

Harmony in Blue and Silver:
Trouville 1865
Oil paint on canvas
49.5 × 75.5

Crepuscule in Flesh Colour
and Green: Valparaiso 1866
Oil paint on canvas
58.6 × 75.9

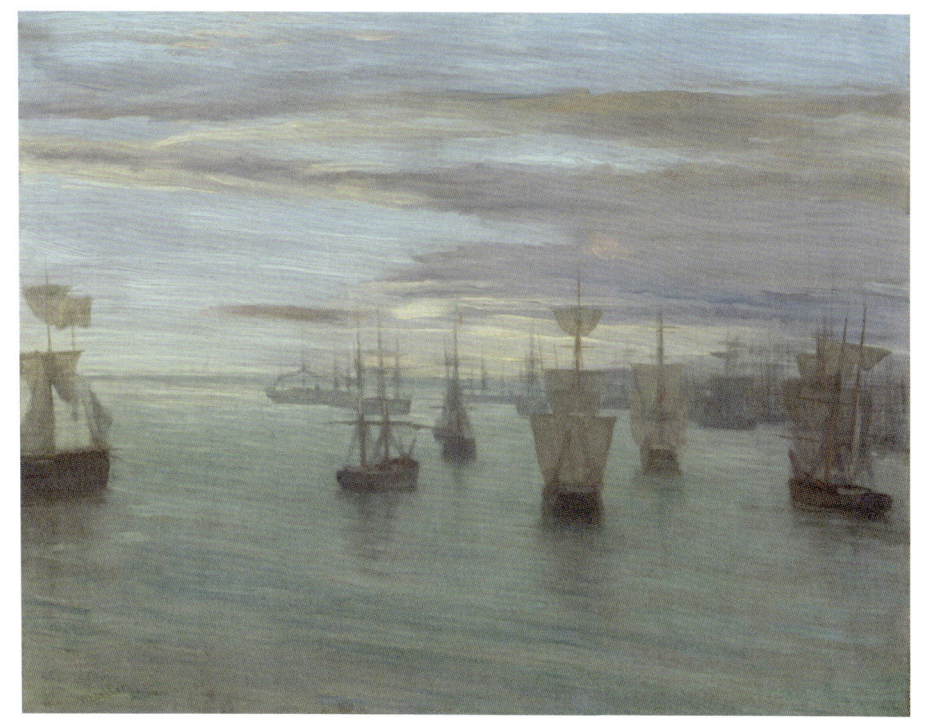

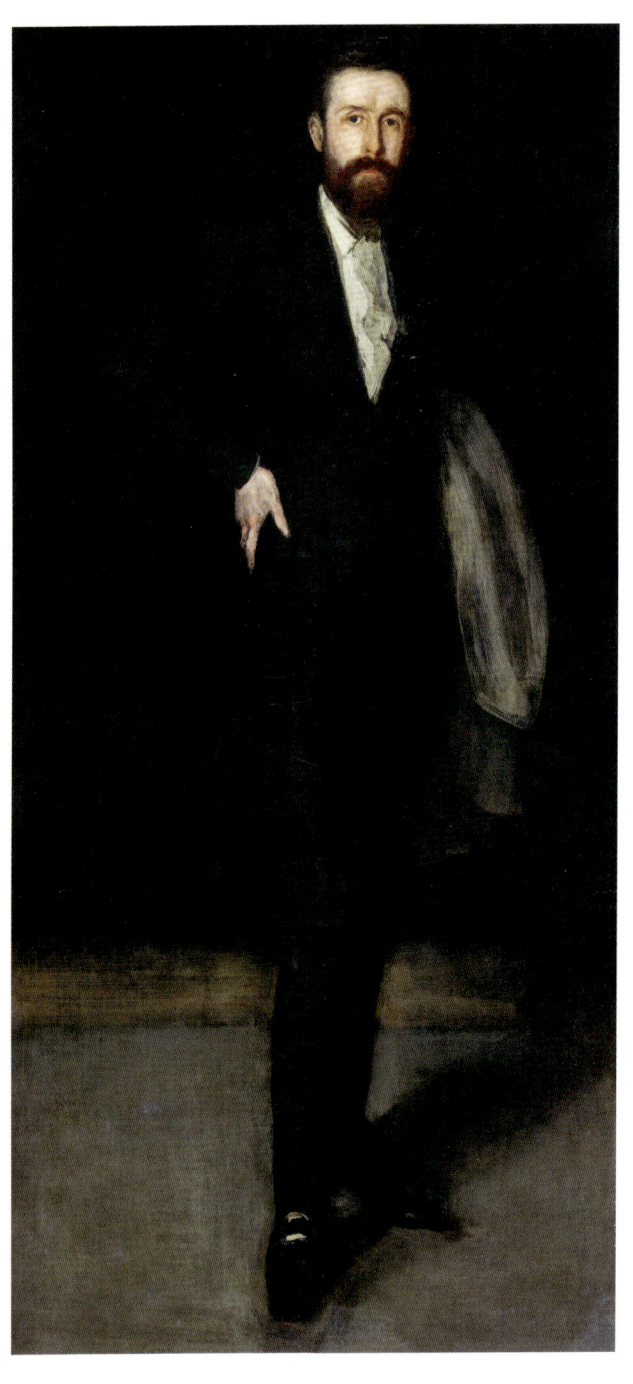

Arrangement in Black: Portrait of F.R. *Leyland* 1870–3
Oil paint on canvas
192.8 × 91.9

Arrangement in Grey and Black,
No.2: Portrait of Thomas
Carlyle 1871–2
Oil paint on canvas
171.1 × 143.5

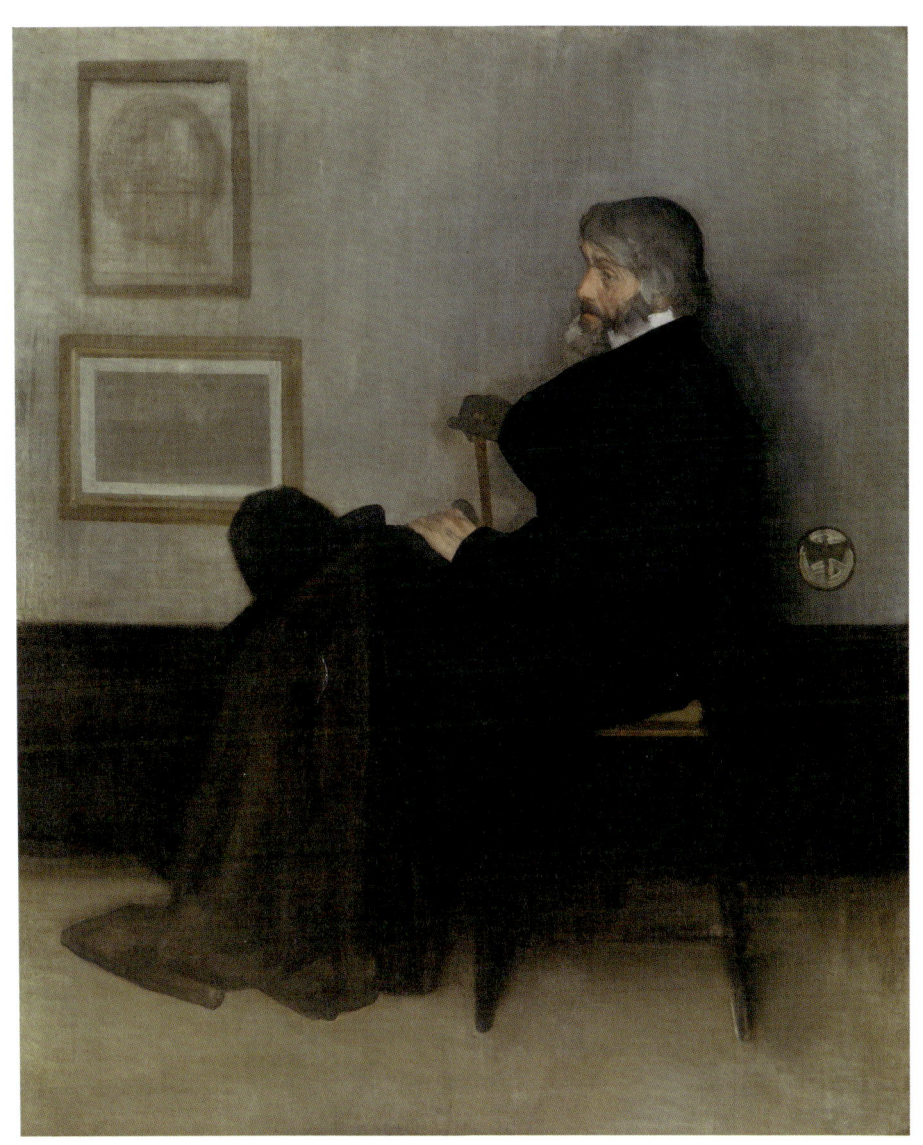

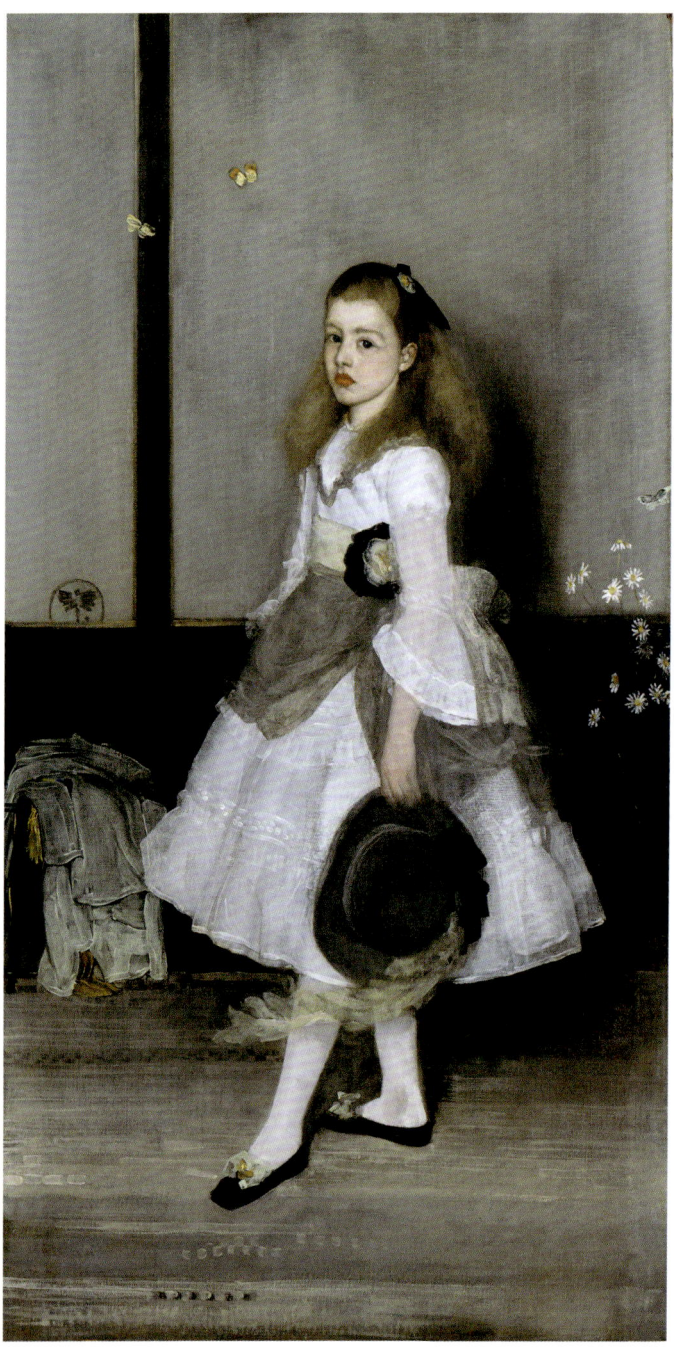

Harmony in Grey and Green:
Miss Cicely Alexander c.1872–4
Oil paint on canvas
190.2 × 97.8

Symphony in Flesh Colour and
Pink: Portrait of Mrs Frances
Leyland 1871–4
Oil paint on canvas
195.9 × 102.2

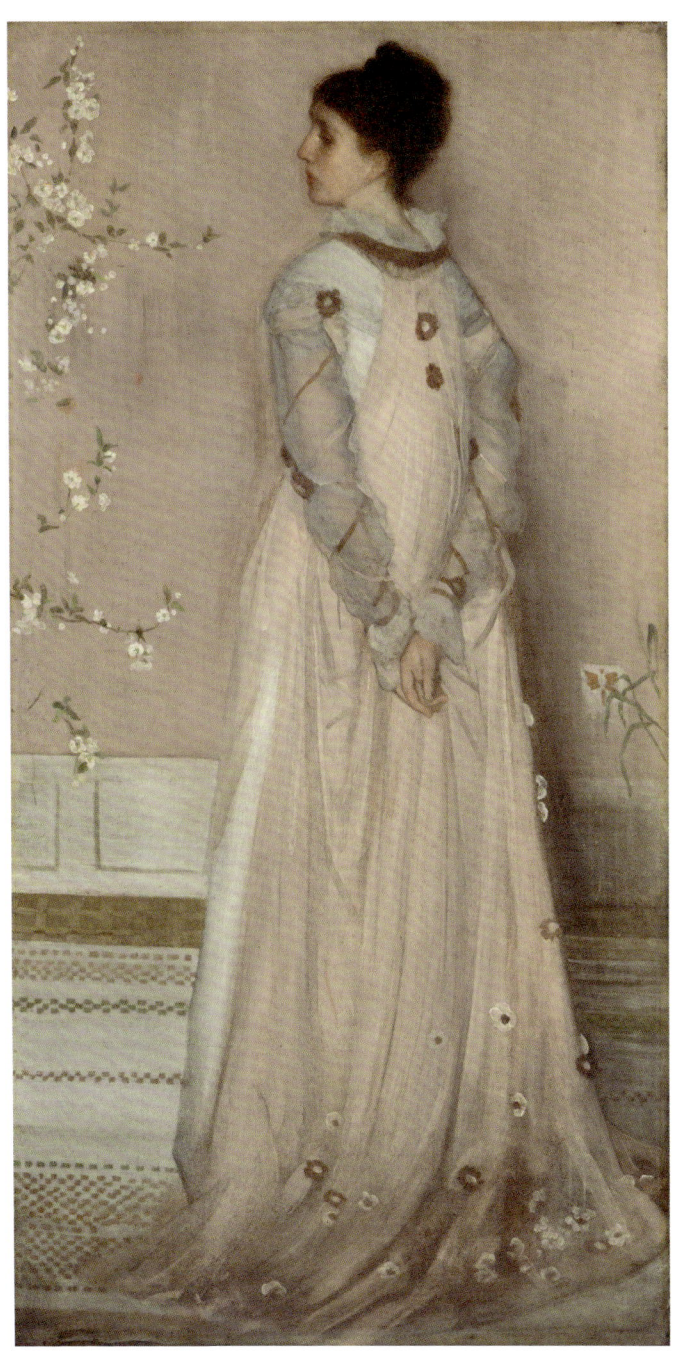

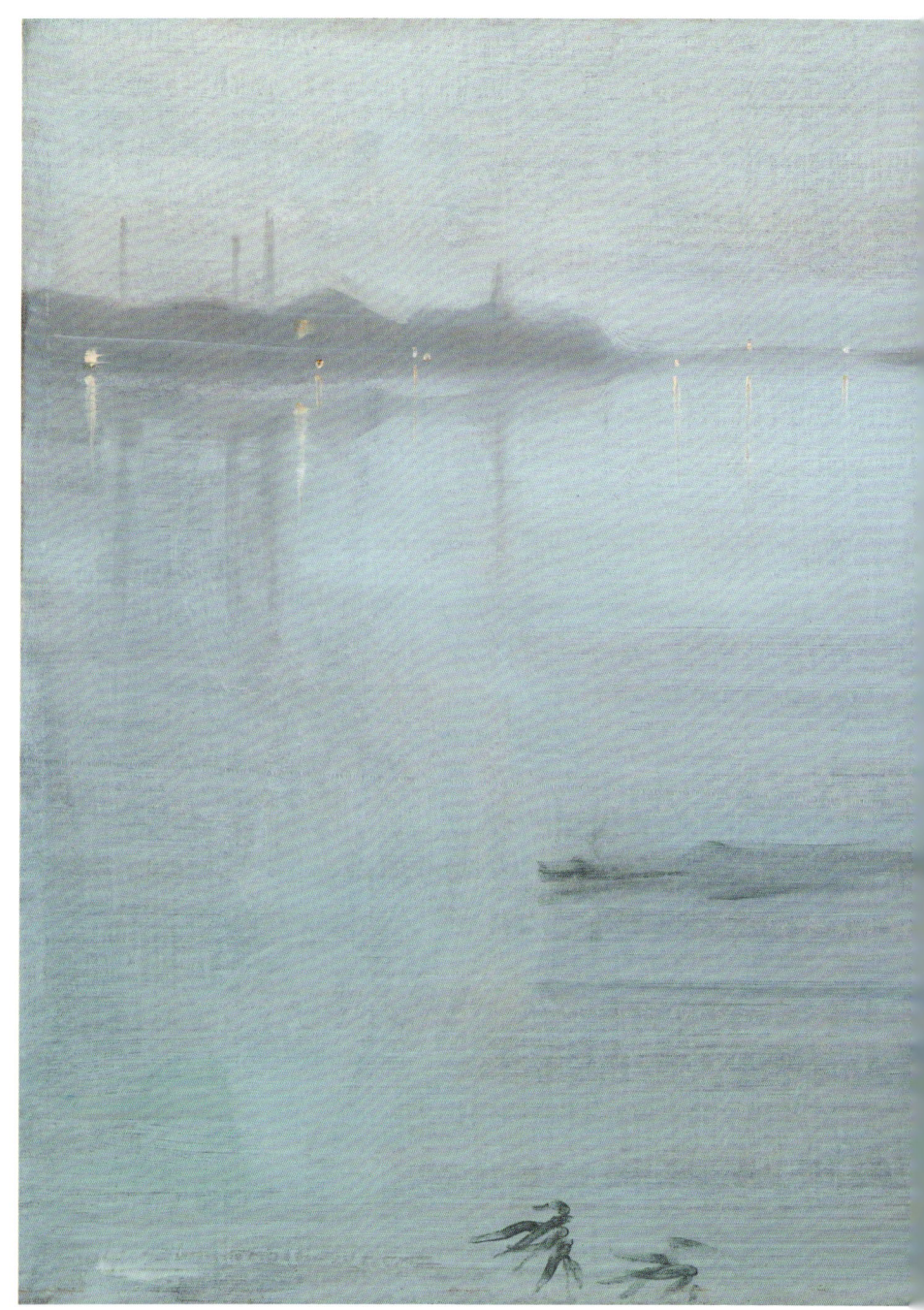

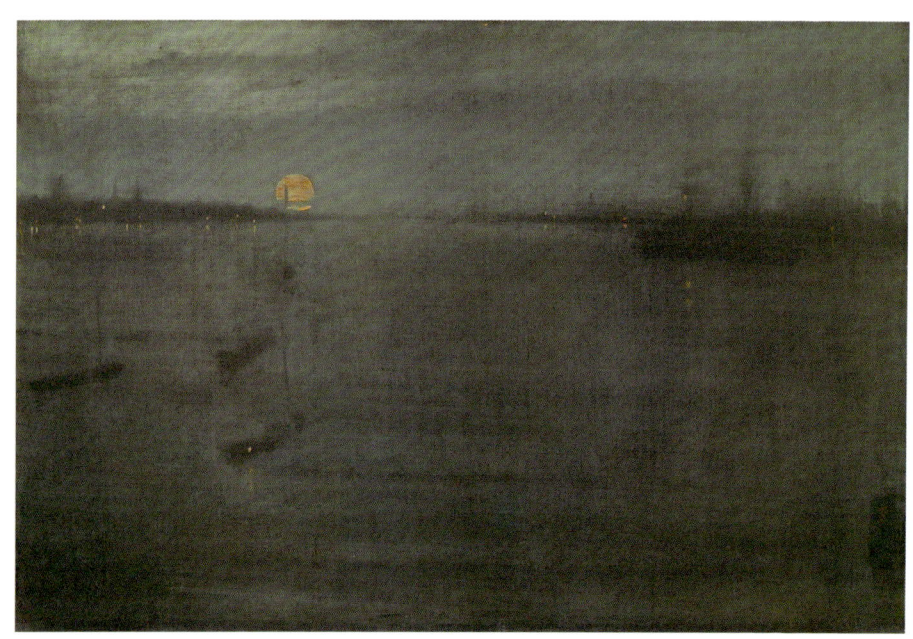

Nocturne: Blue and Gold –
Southampton Water 1872
Oil paint on canvas
50.3 × 76

Nocturne: Blue and Gold –
Battersea Bridge c.1872–5
Oil paint on canvas
68.3 × 51.2

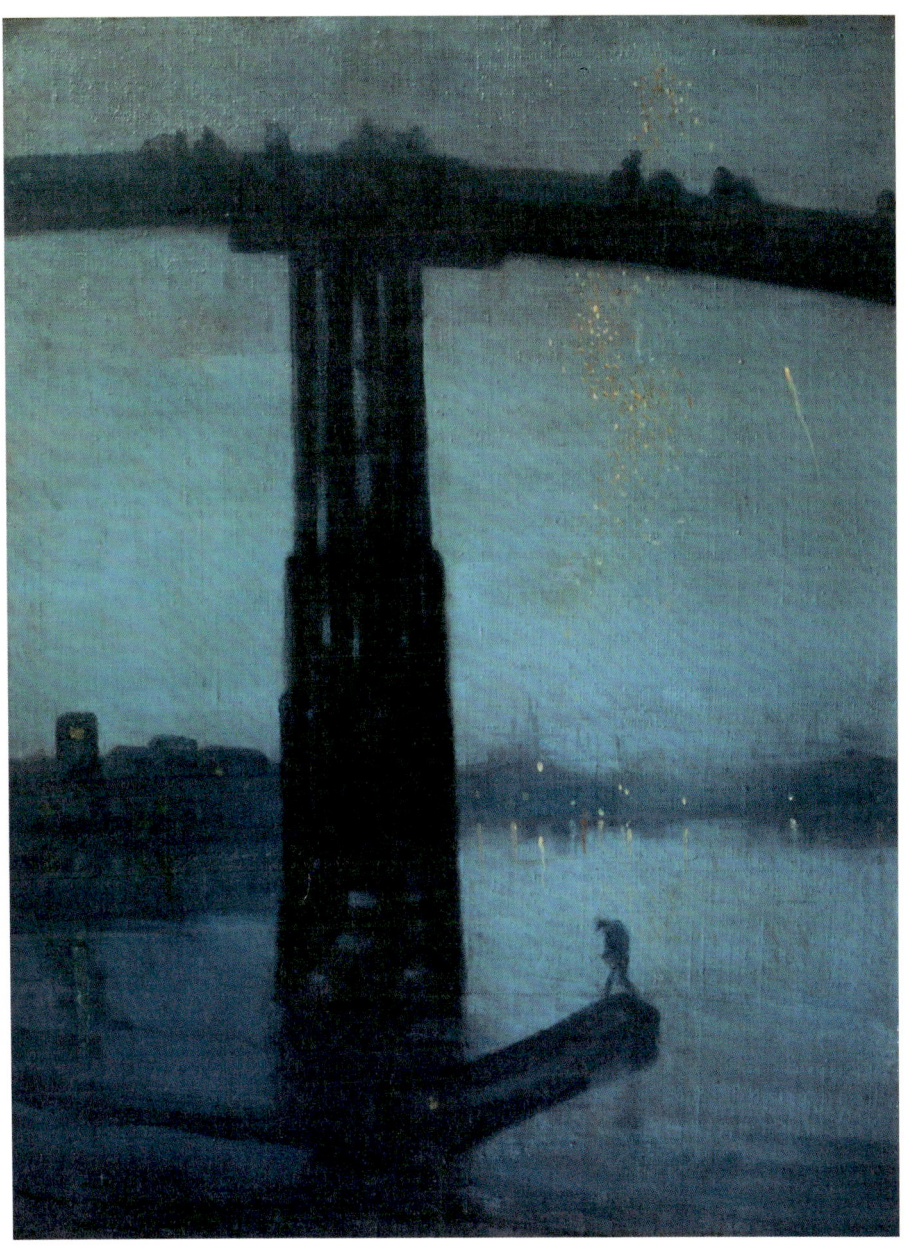

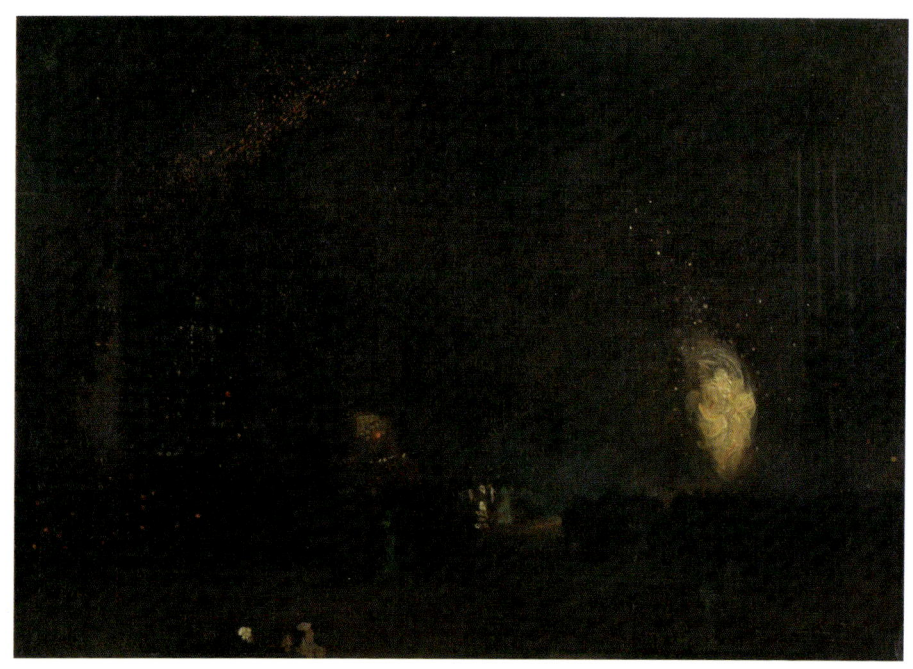

Nocturne: Black and Gold –
The Fire Wheel 1875
Oil paint on canvas
54.3 × 76.2

Nocturne in Black and Gold:
The Falling Rocket 1875
Oil paint on canvas
60.3 × 46.6

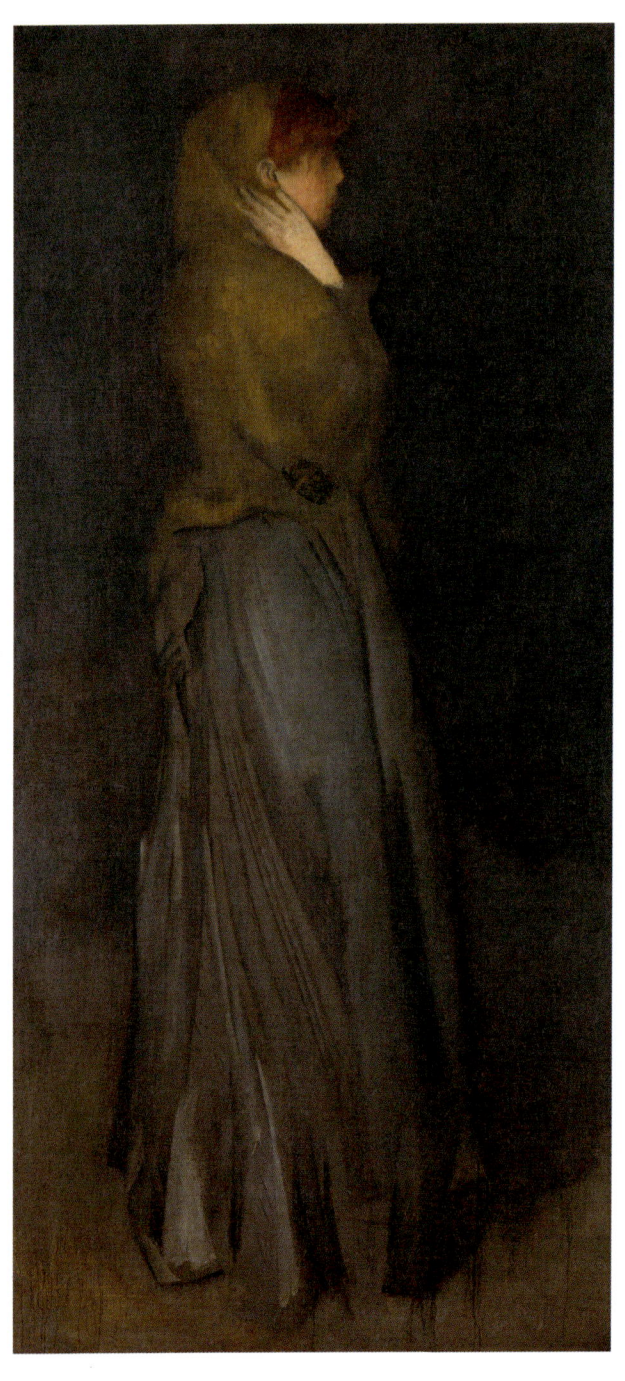

Arrangement in Yellow and Grey: Effie Deans 1876–7
Oil paint on canvas
194 × 93

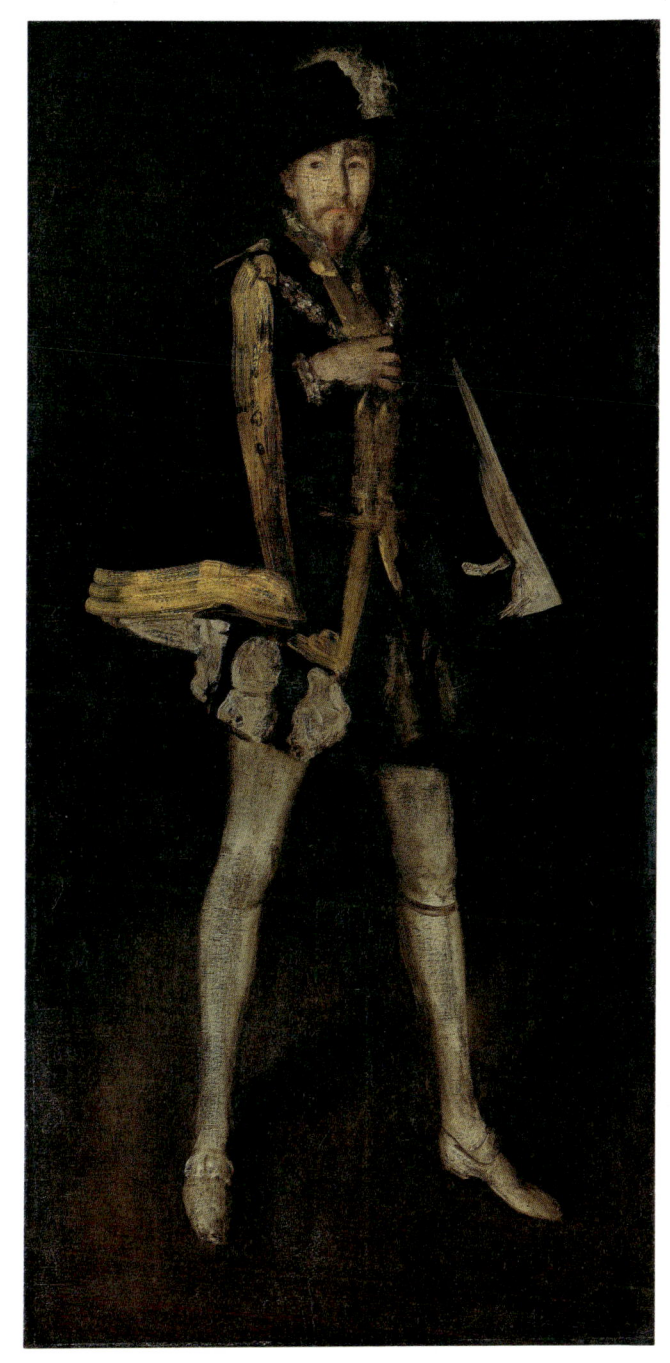

Arrangement in Black, No.3:
Sir Henry Irving as Philip II
of Spain 1876
Oil paint on canvas
215.3 × 108.6

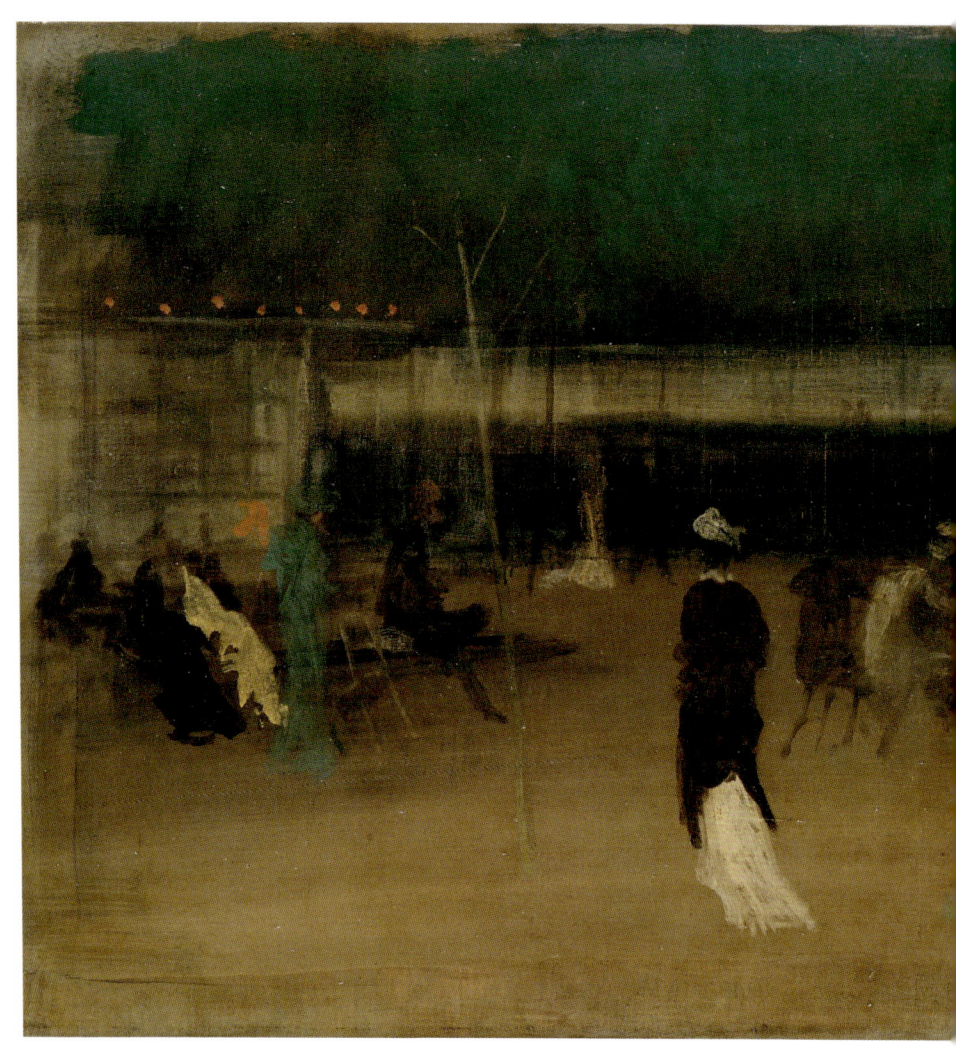

Cremorne Gardens, No.2
1875–7
Oil paint on canvas
68.5 × 135.5

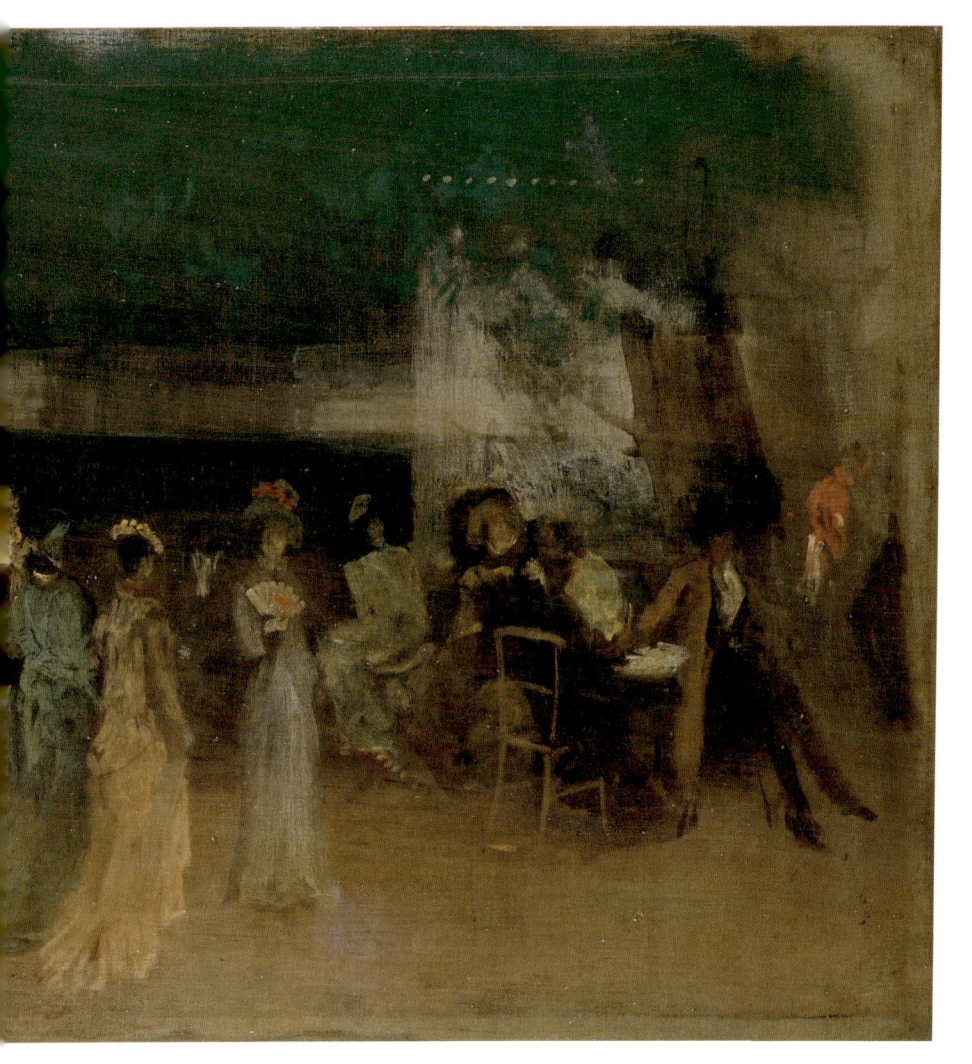

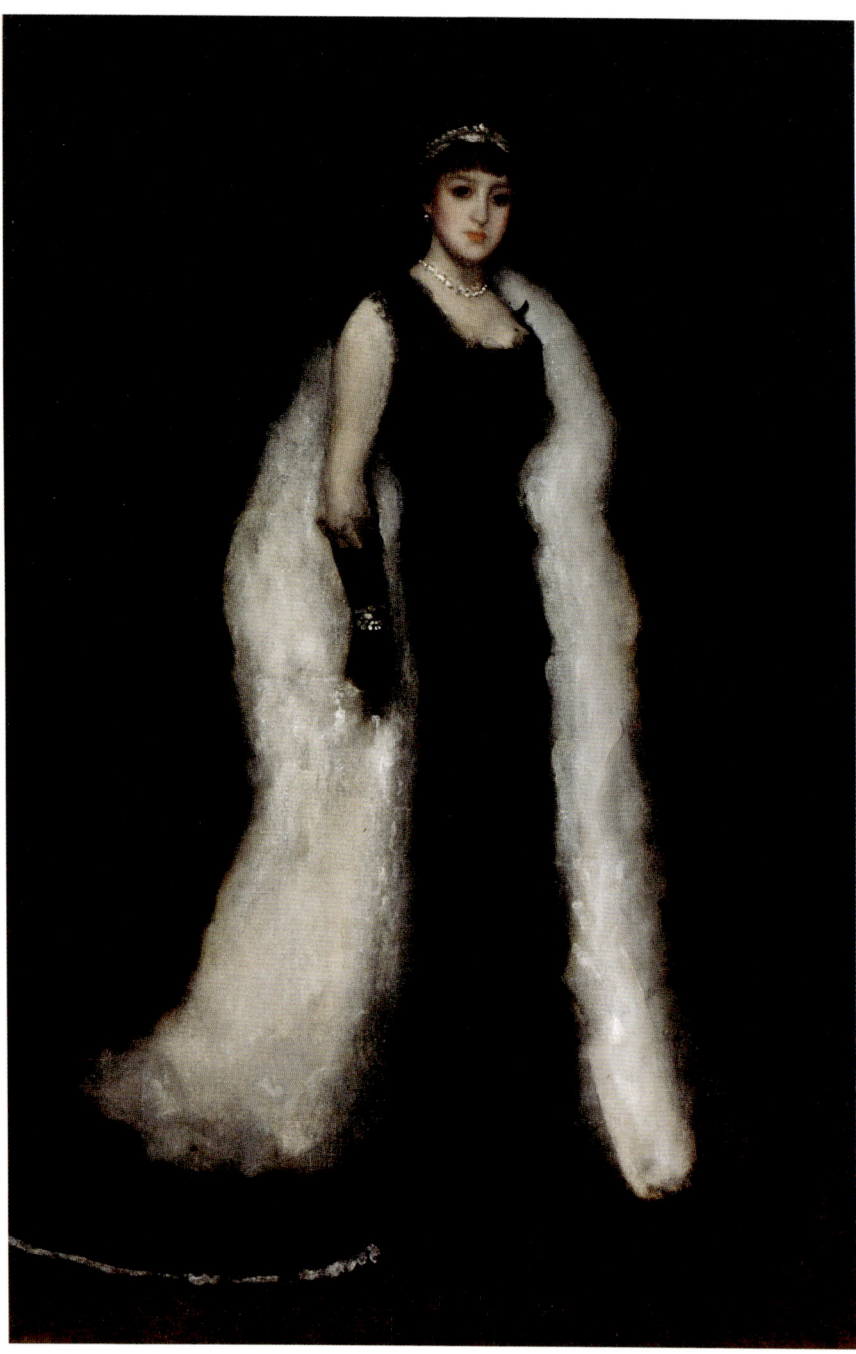

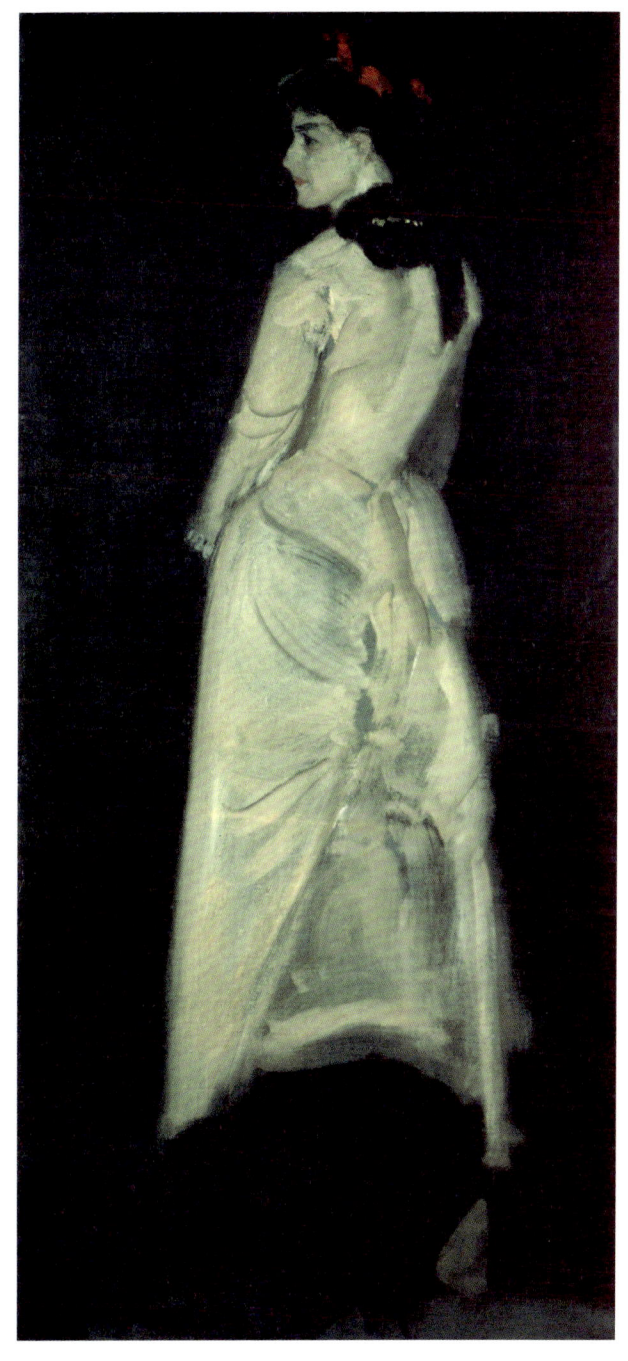

Arrangement in Black:
Lady Meux 1881–2
Oil paint on canvas
194.3 × 130.2

Harmony in Flesh Colour and
Black: Portrait of Mrs Louise
Jopling 1877–8
Oil paint on canvas
192.5 × 90

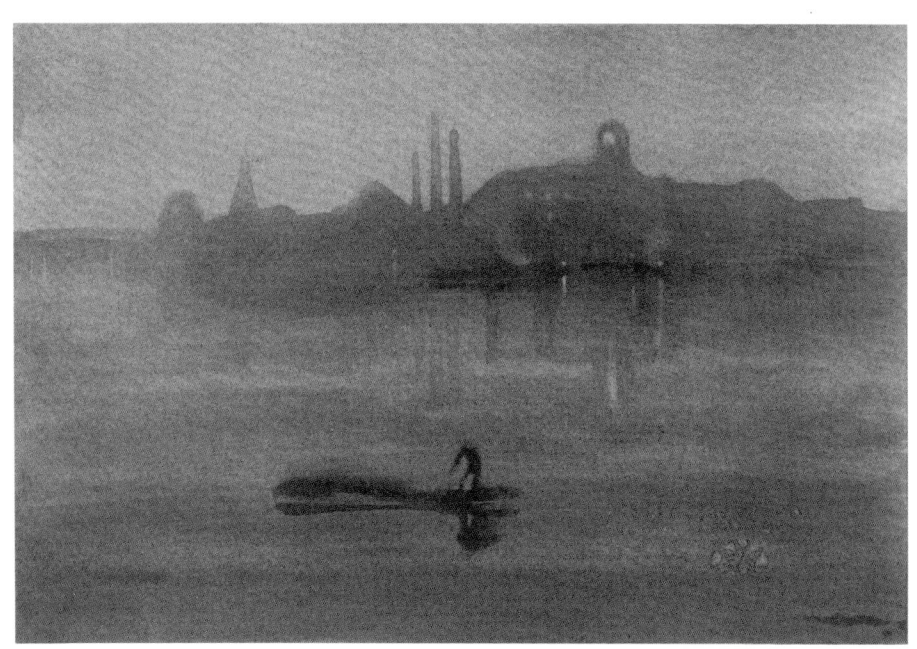

Nocturne 1878
Lithotint on paper
17.1 × 25.9

The Little Venice 1880
Etching on paper
18.5 × 26.4

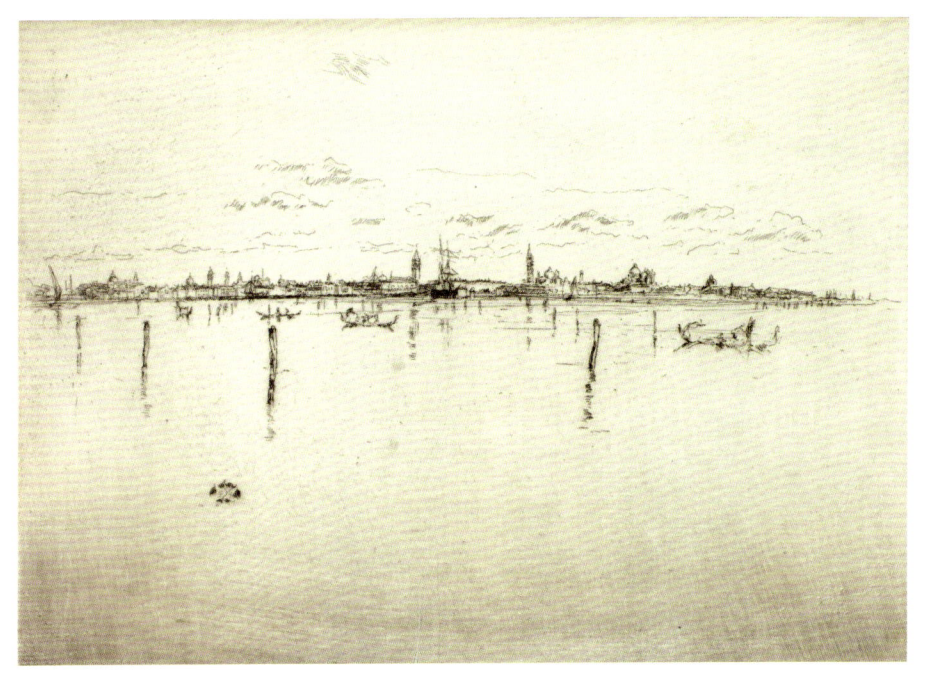

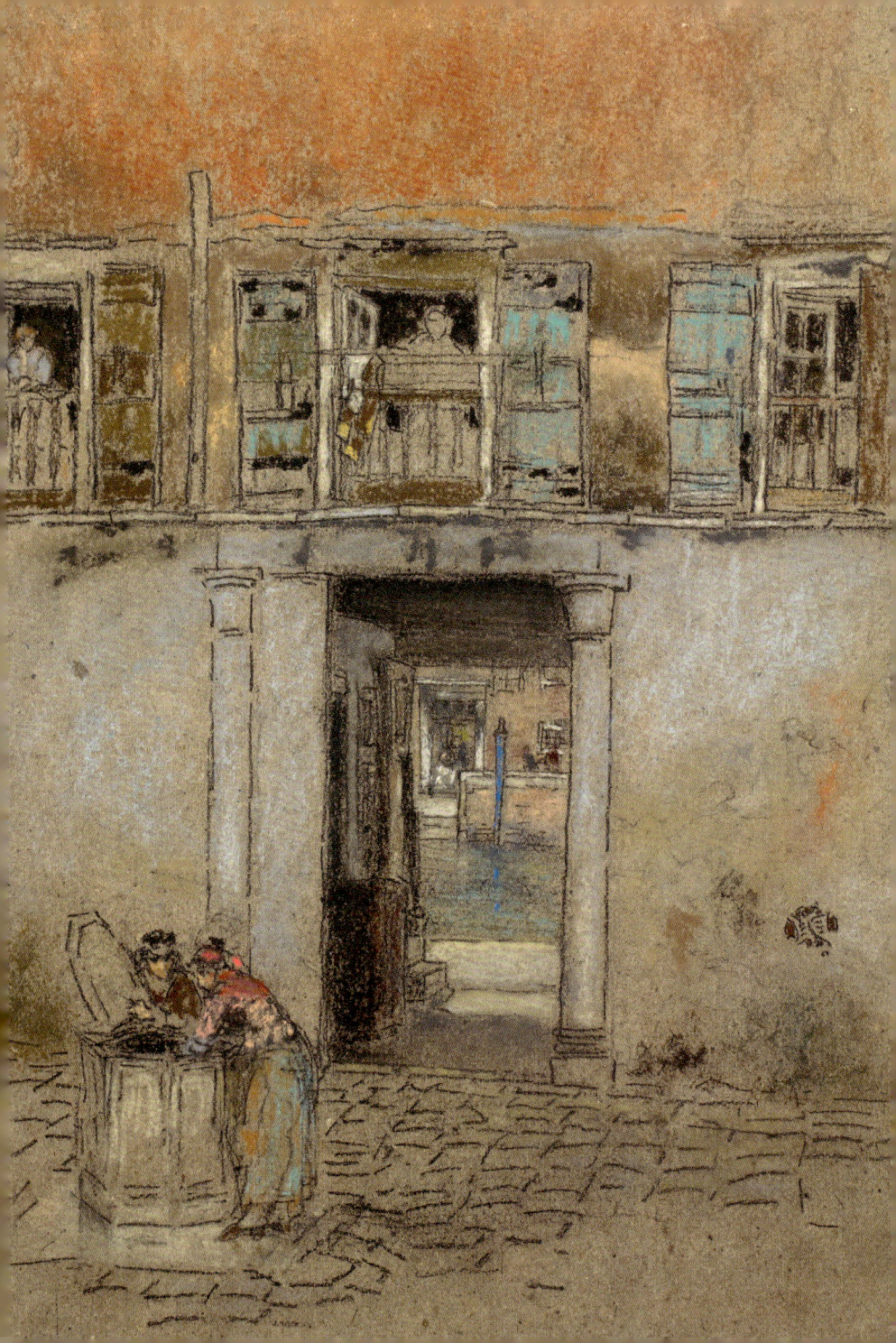

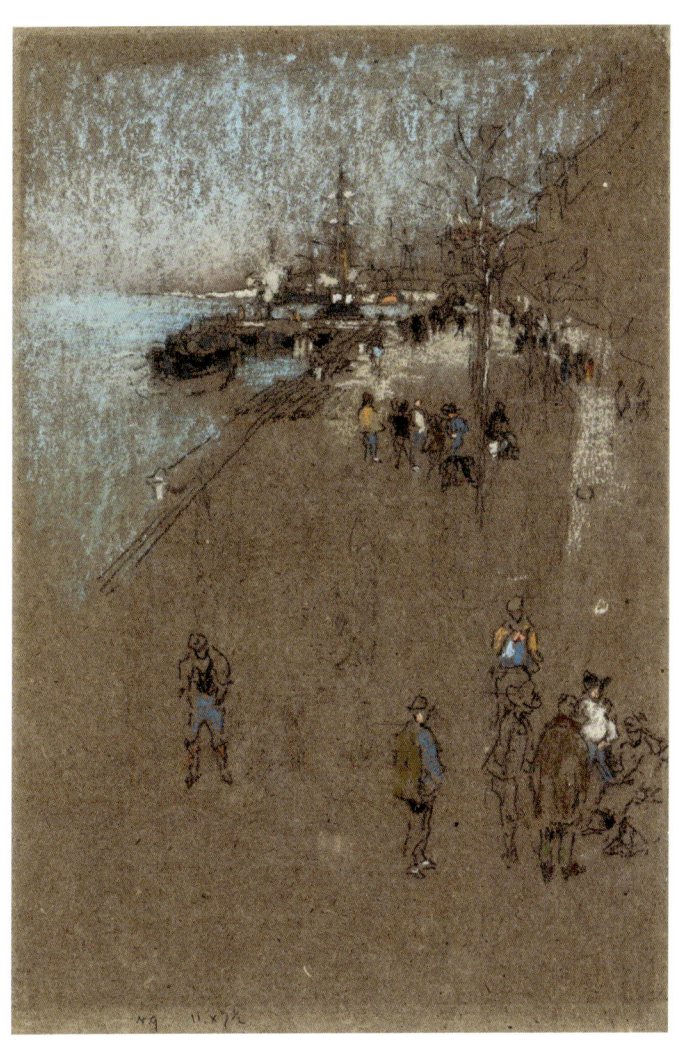

*Courtyard on Canal: Grey and
Red* 1879–80
Chalk and pastel on paper
30.1 × 20.2

*The Zattere: Harmony in Blue
and Brown* 1879–80
Chalk and pastel on paper
30 × 20.3

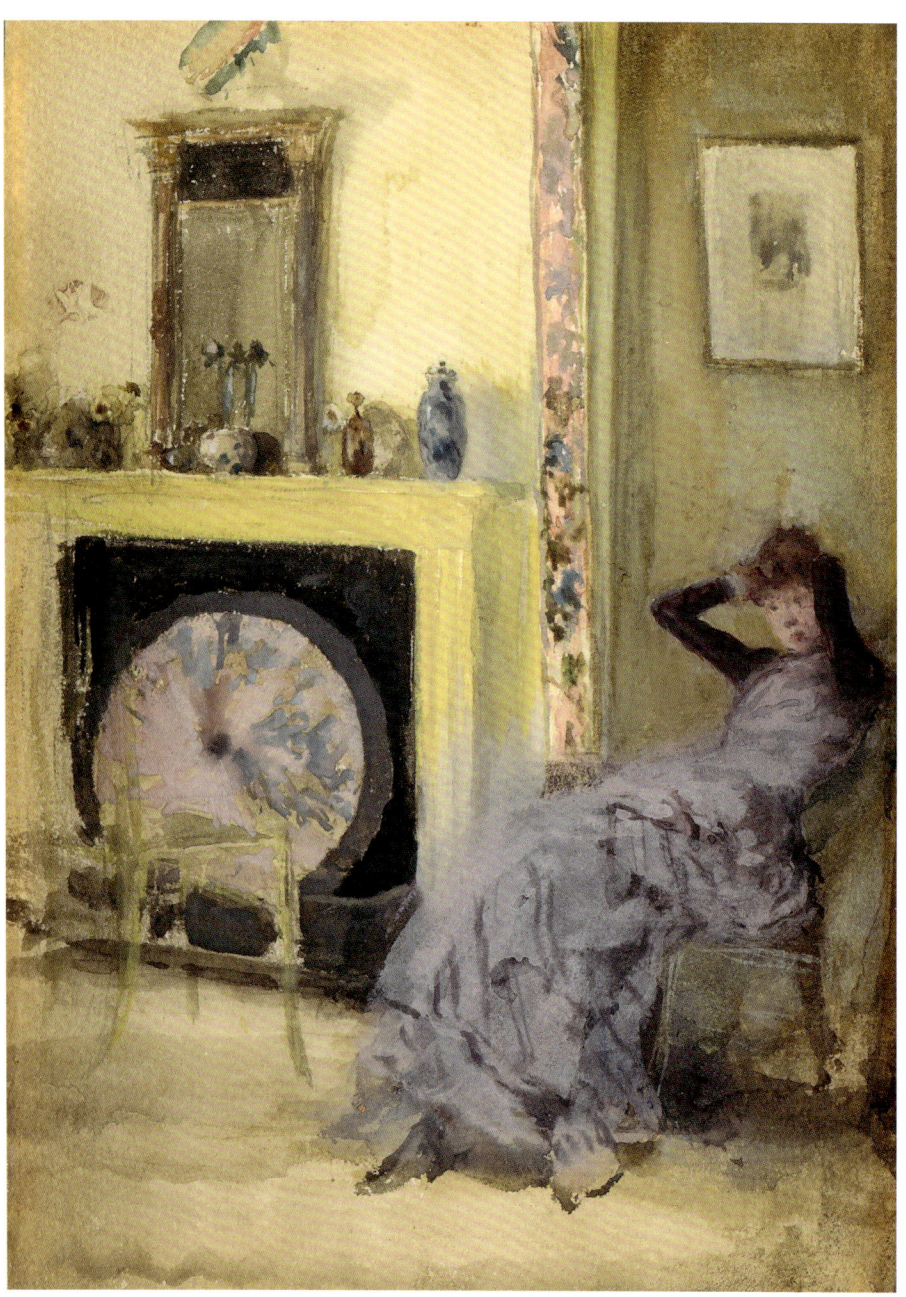

The Yellow Room 1883–4
Watercolour and gouache
on paper
24.8 × 17.8

*Arrangement en couleur chair et
noir: Portrait de Théodore Duret*
1883–5
Oil paint on canvas
193.4 × 90.8

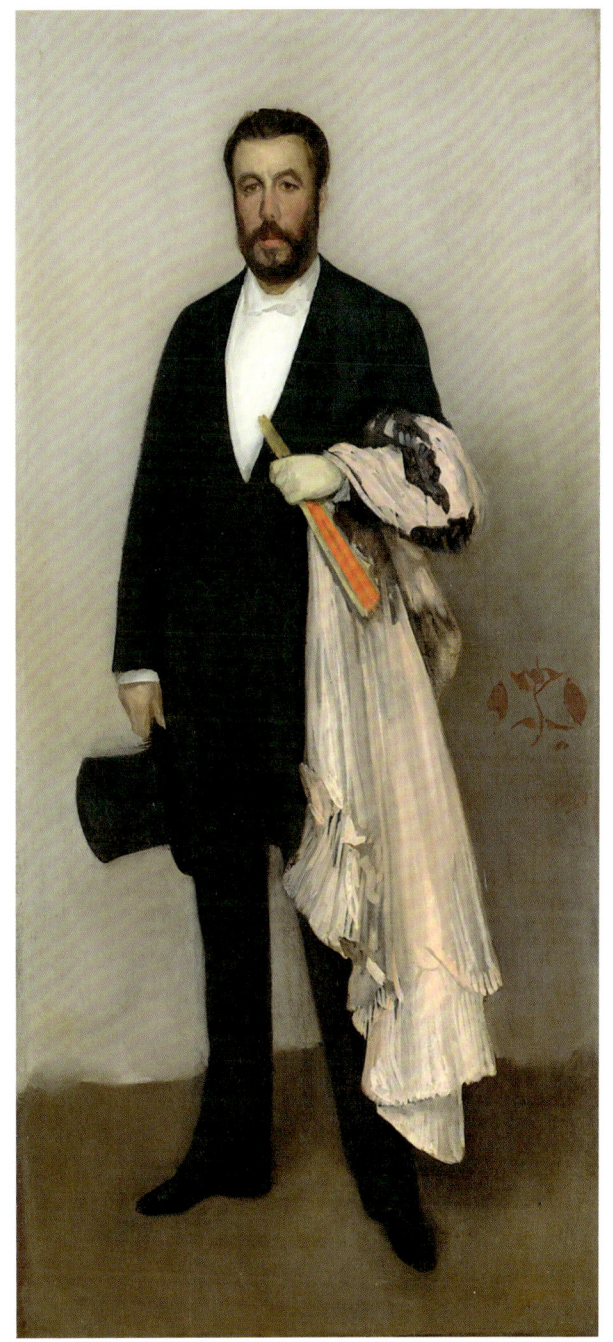

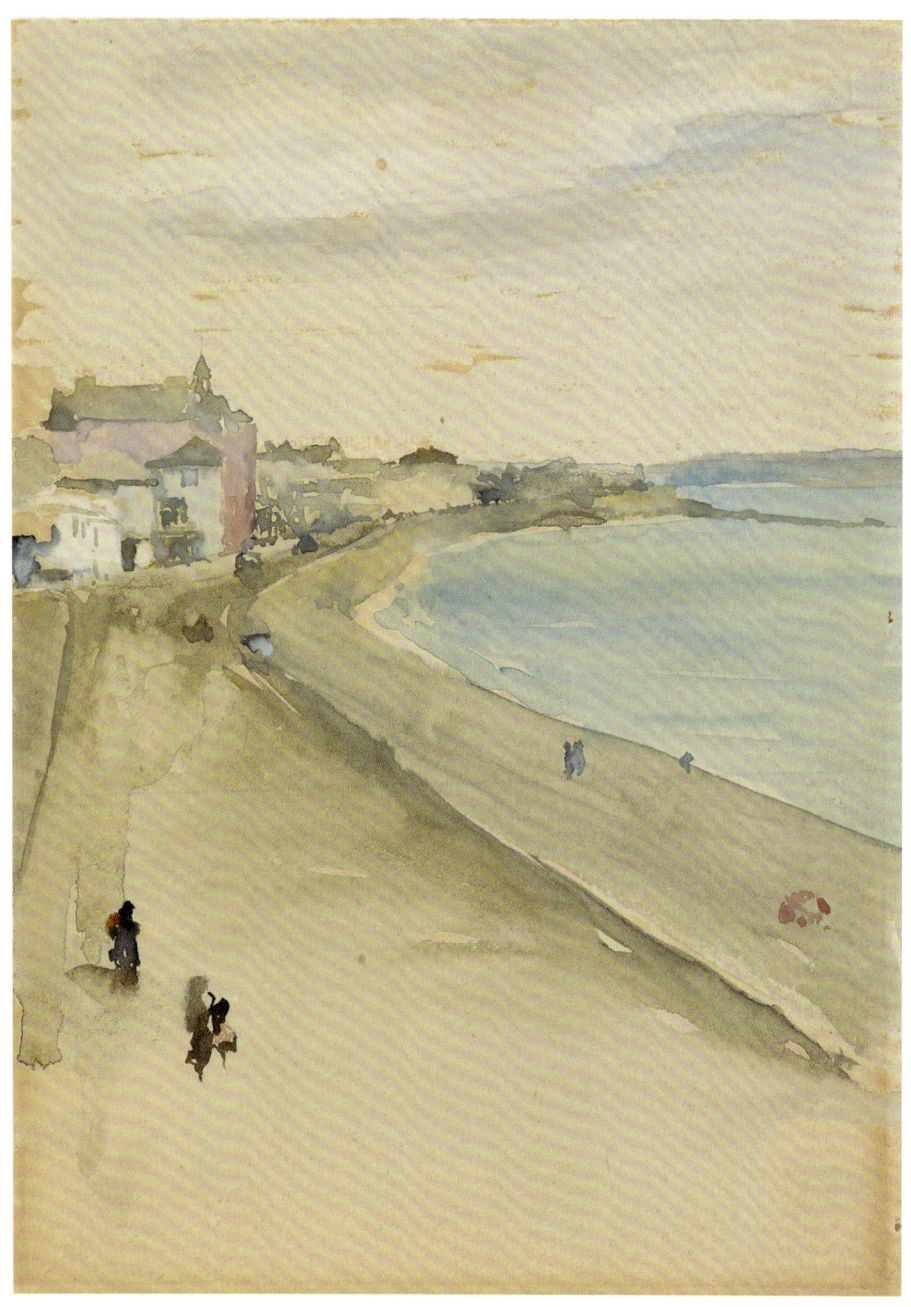

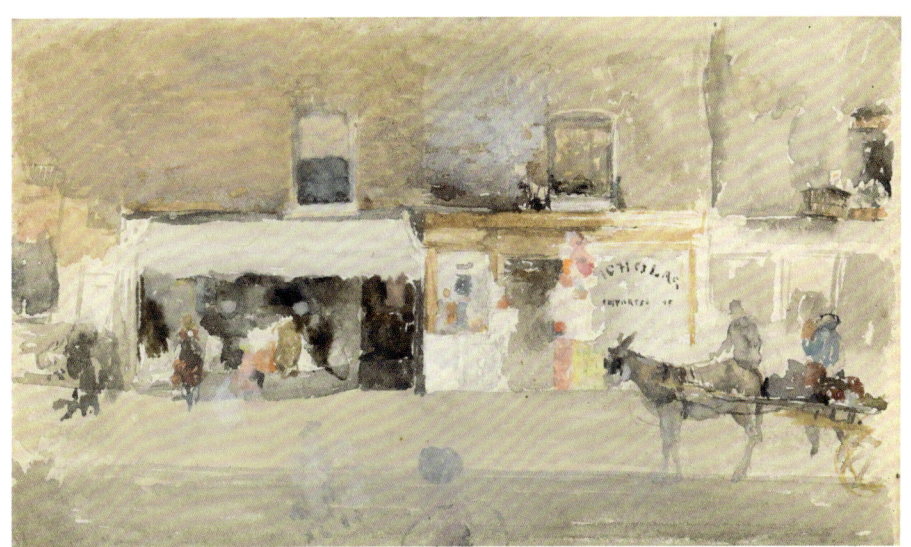

St Ives 1883–4
Watercolour on paper
17.5 × 12.6

A Chelsea Street 1883–6
Watercolour on paper
12.6 × 21.7

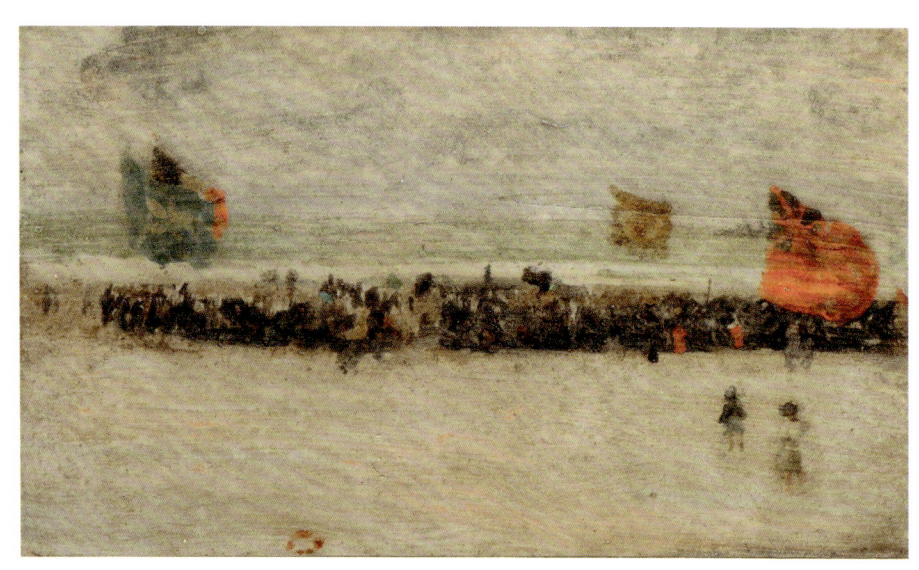

A Red Note: *Fête on the Sands,*
Ostend 1887
Oil paint on wood
13.7 × 23.5

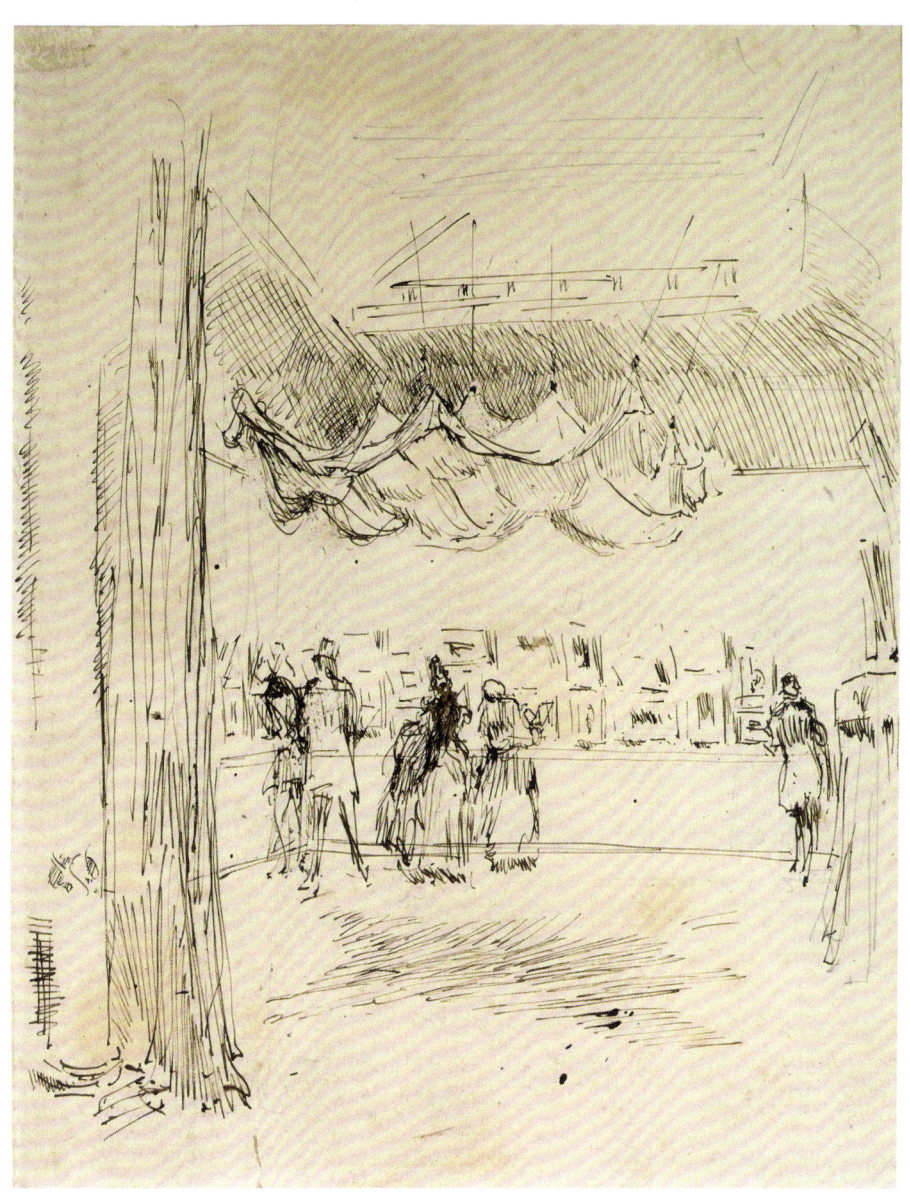

*Sketch of the Interior of the
Suffolk Street Gallery during an
Exhibition 1886–7*
Ink and graphite on paper
20 × 15.8

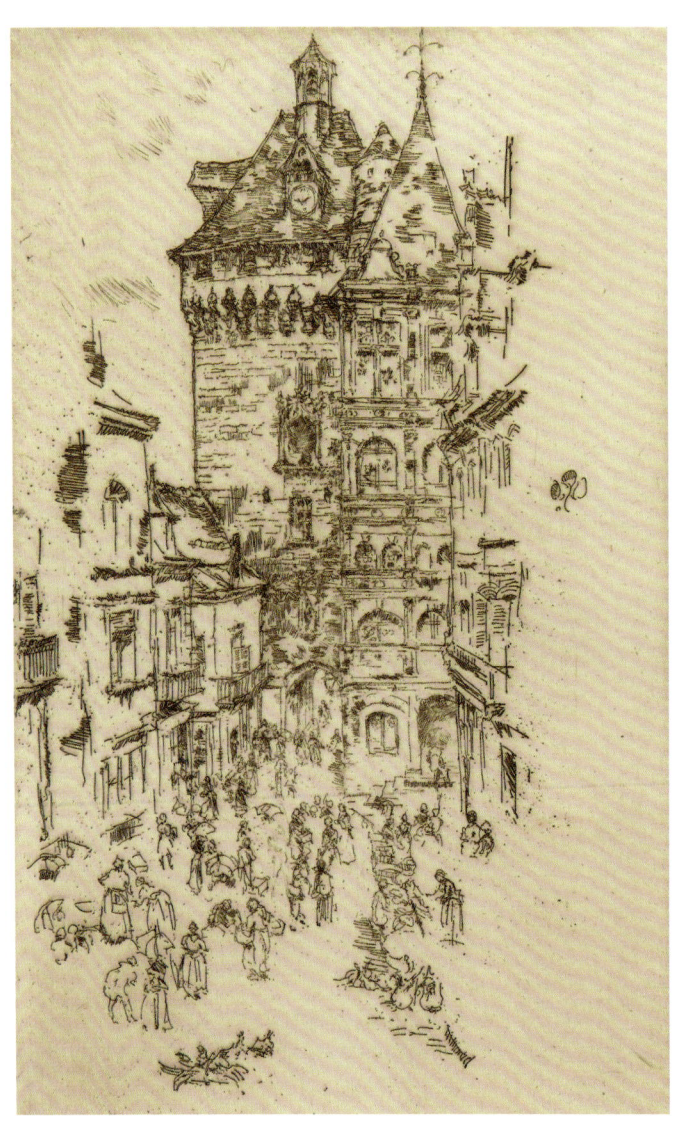

Hôtel de Ville, Loches 1888
Etching and drypoint on
paper
27 × 16.5

The Long Balcony 1894
Lithograph on paper
20.4 × 15.8

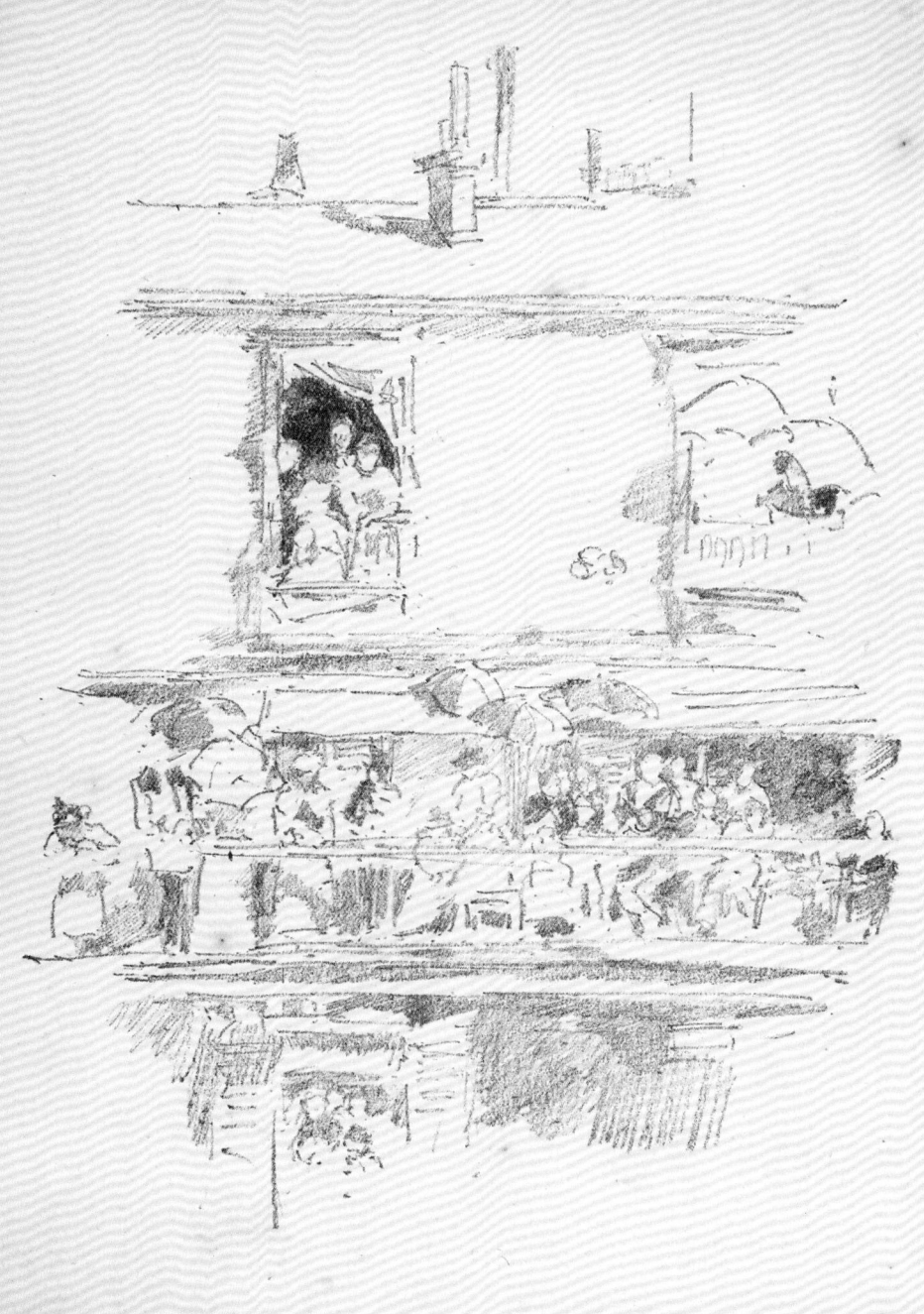

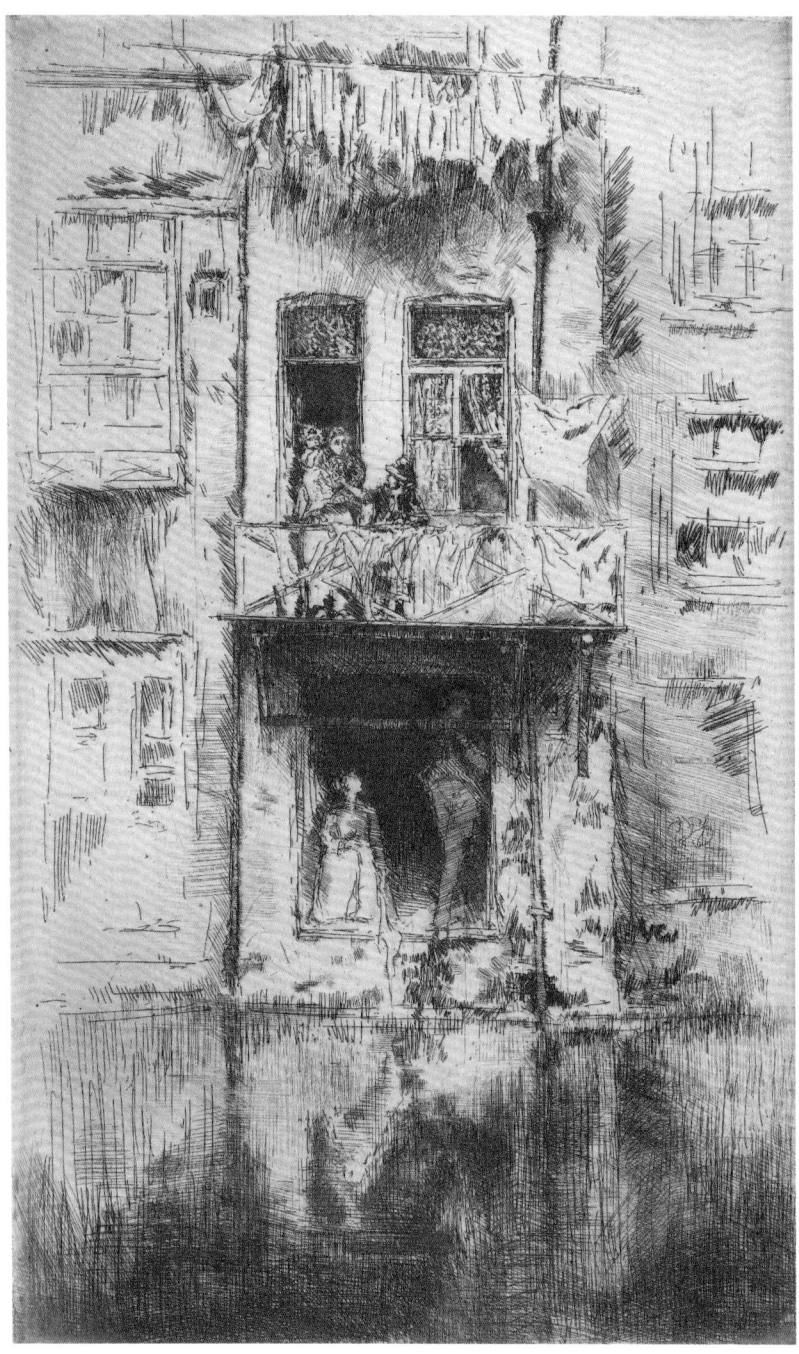

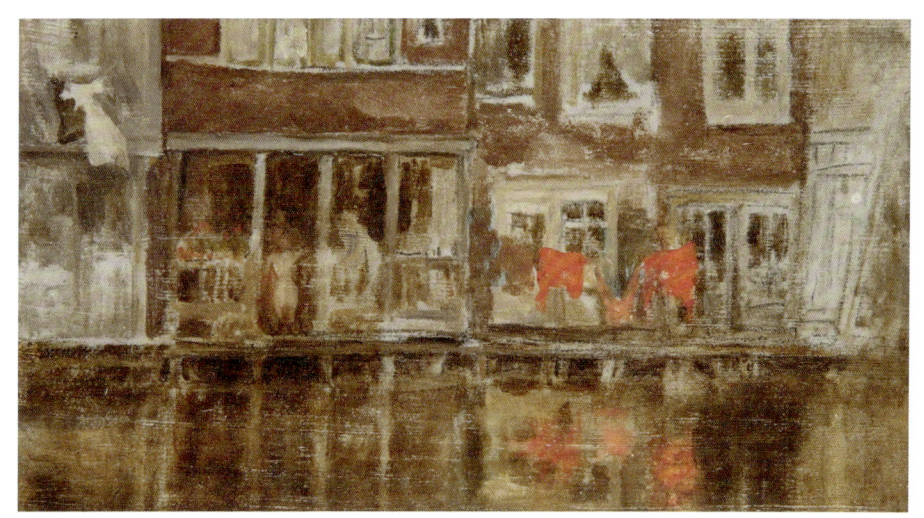

Balcony, Amsterdam 1889
Etching and drypoint on
paper
27.2 × 16.9

The Canal, Amsterdam 1889
Oil paint on wood
13.8 × 23.2

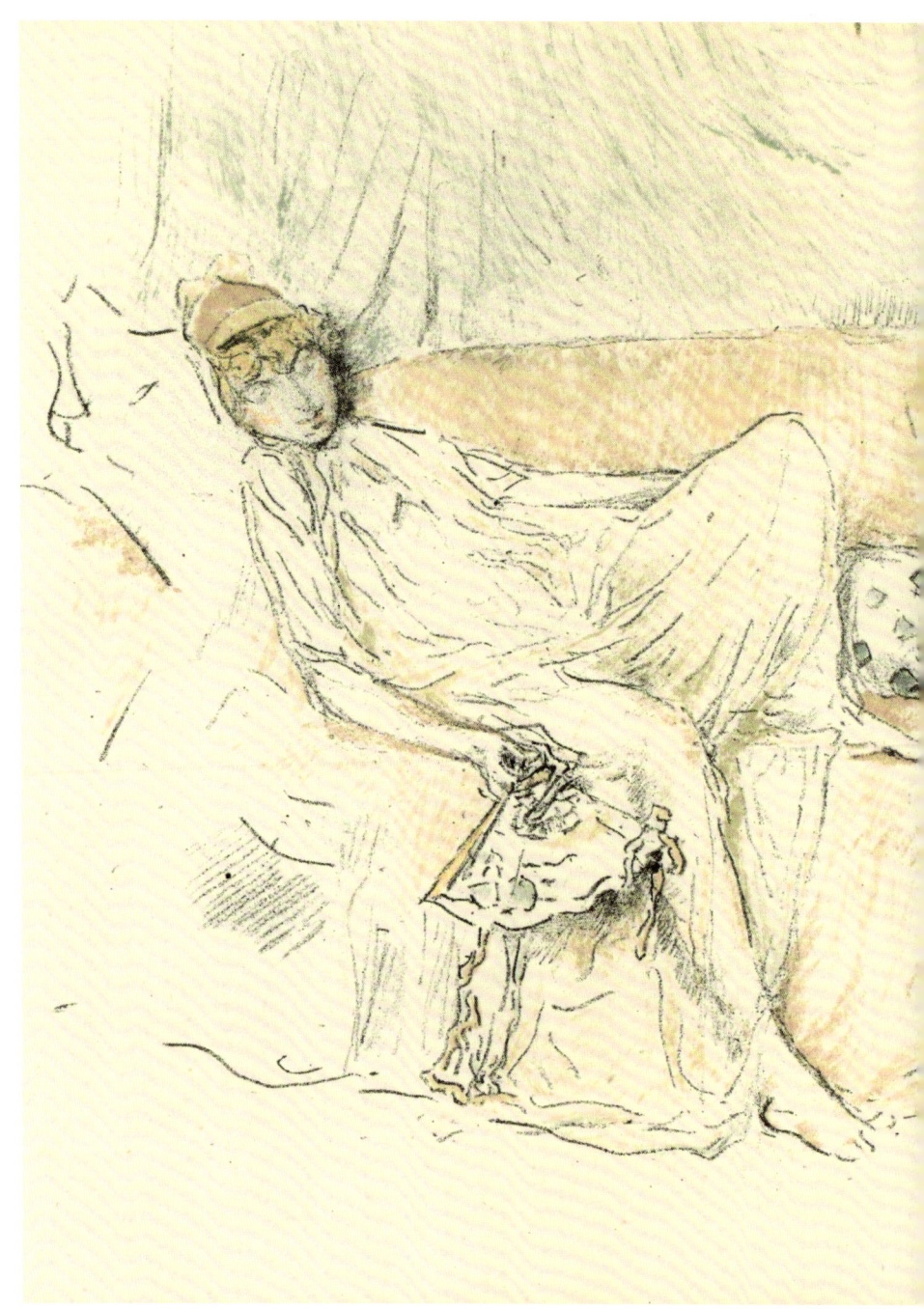

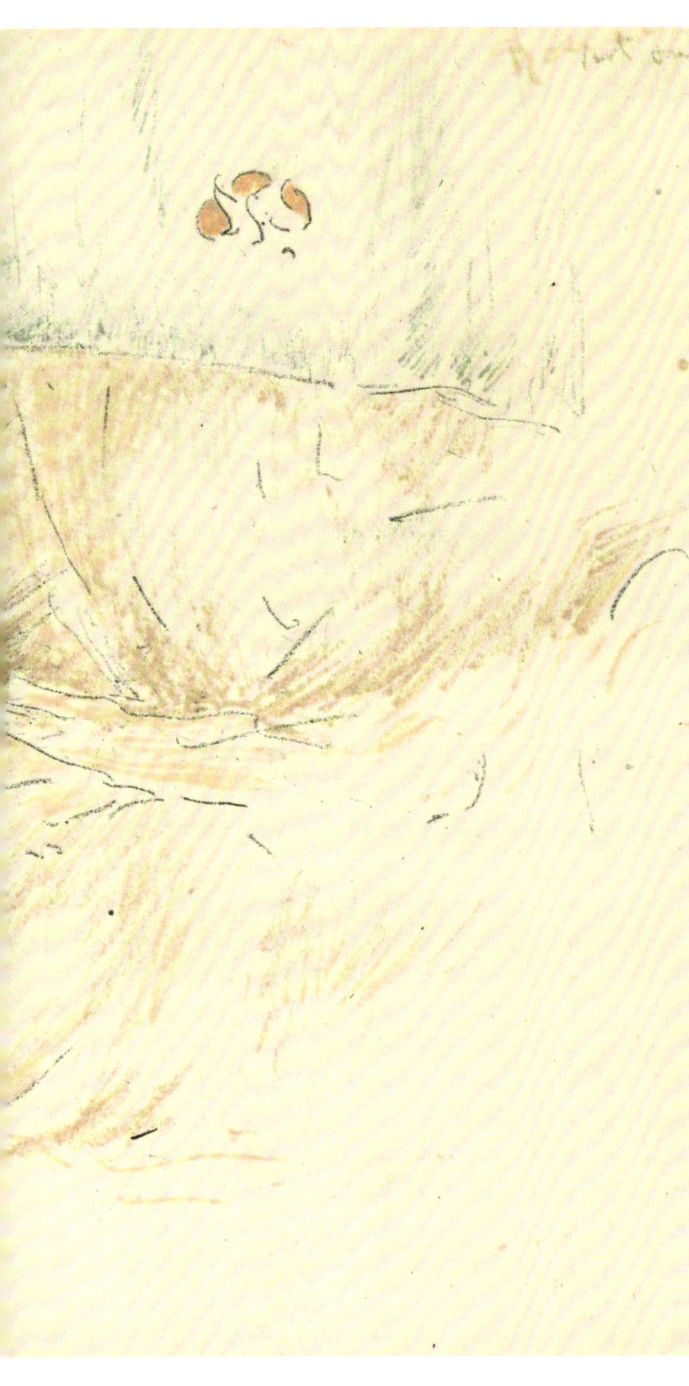

Draped Figure, Reclining 1892
Lithograph on paper
18 × 25.8

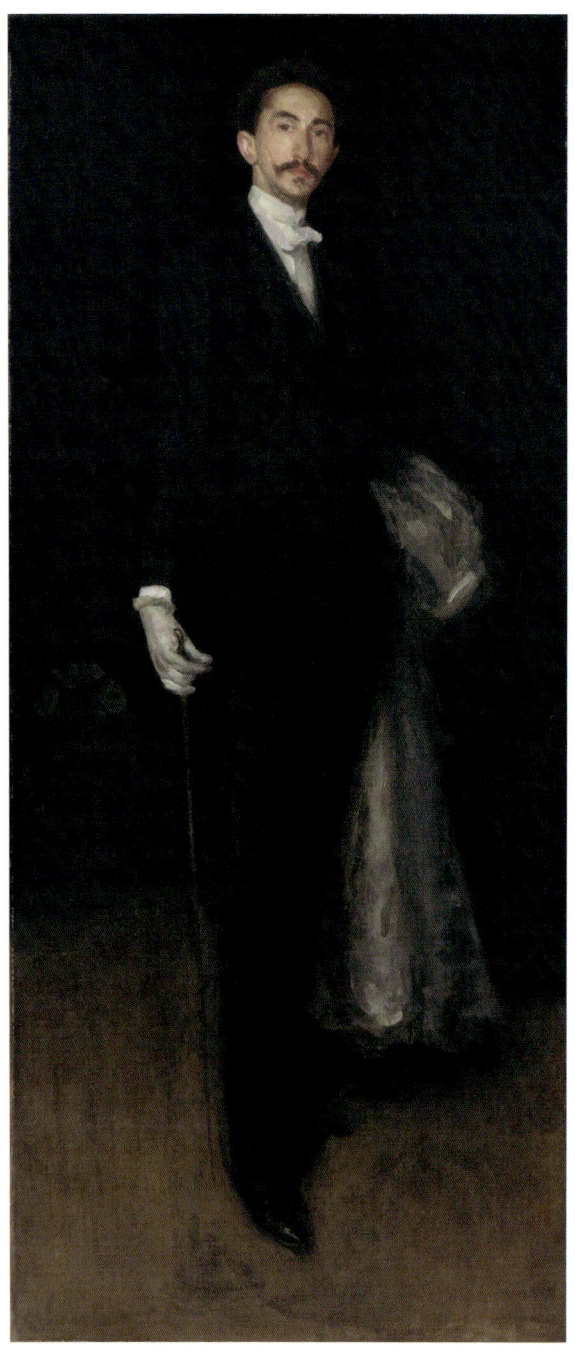

*Arrangement in Black and Gold:
Comte Robert de Montesquiou-
Fezensac* 1891–2
Oil paint on canvas
208.6 × 91.8

Stéphane Mallarmé 1892
Lithograph on paper
9.7 × 7

OVERLEAF
Violet and Silver: A Deep Sea
1893
Oil paint on canvas
50.2 × 73.3

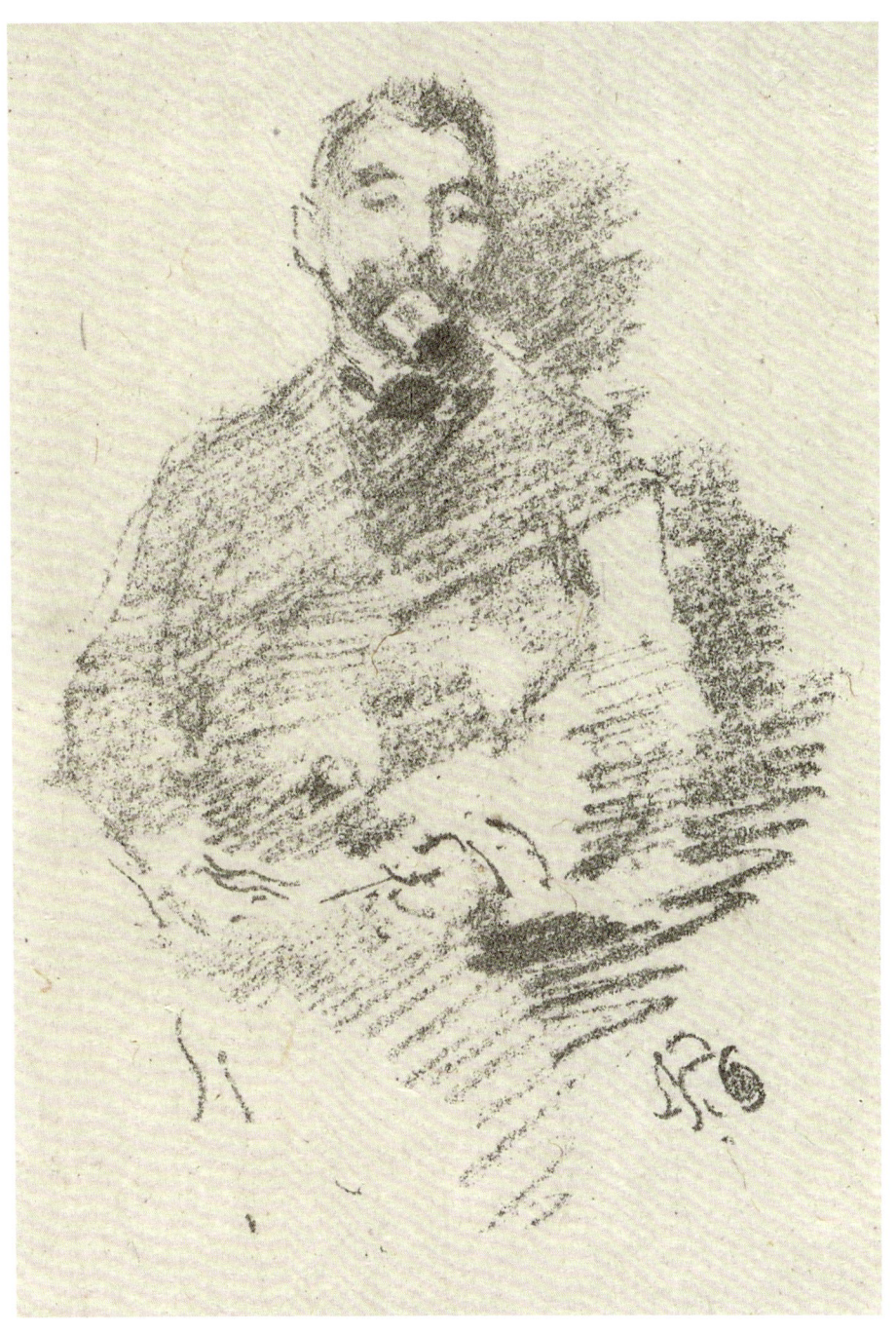

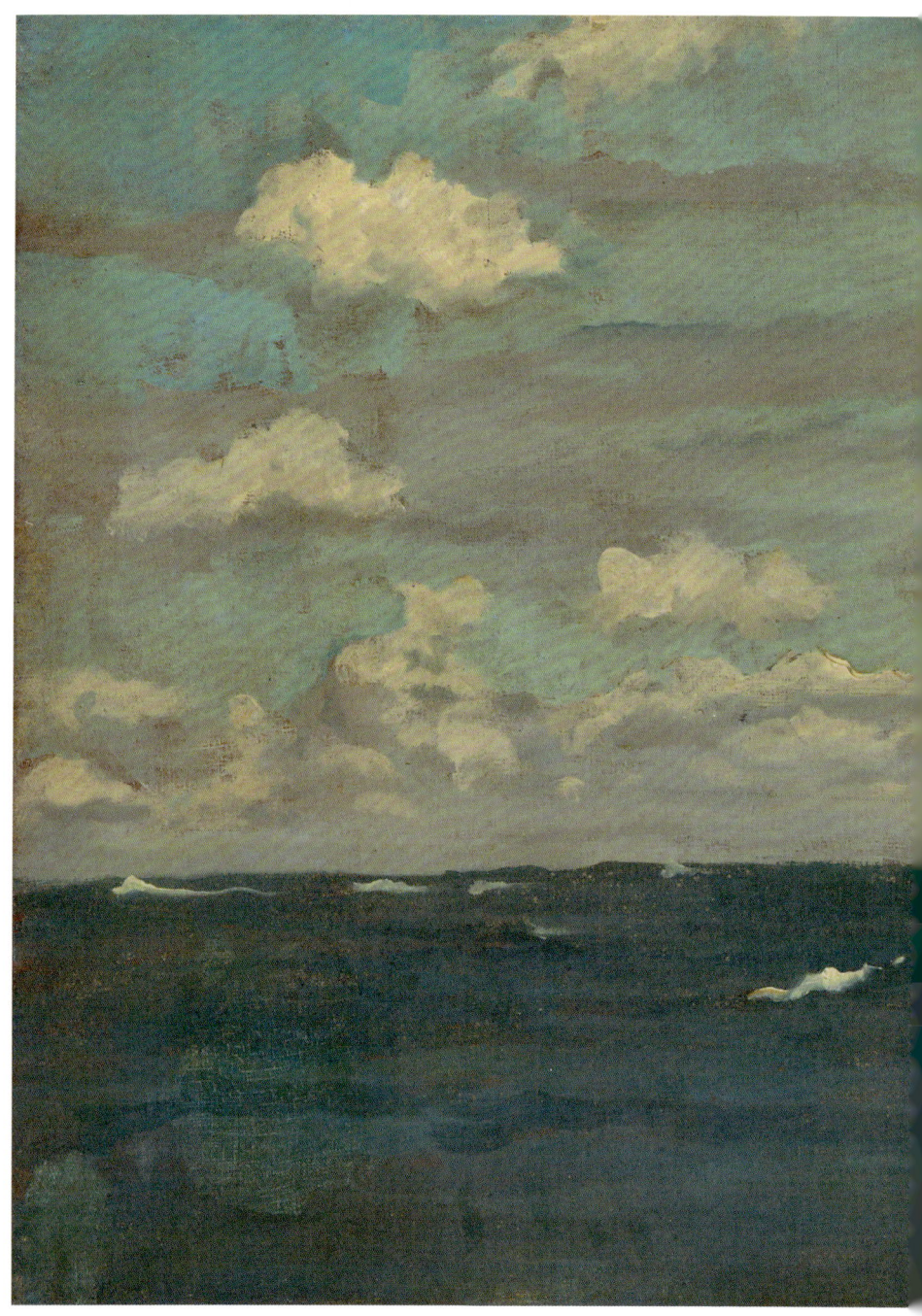

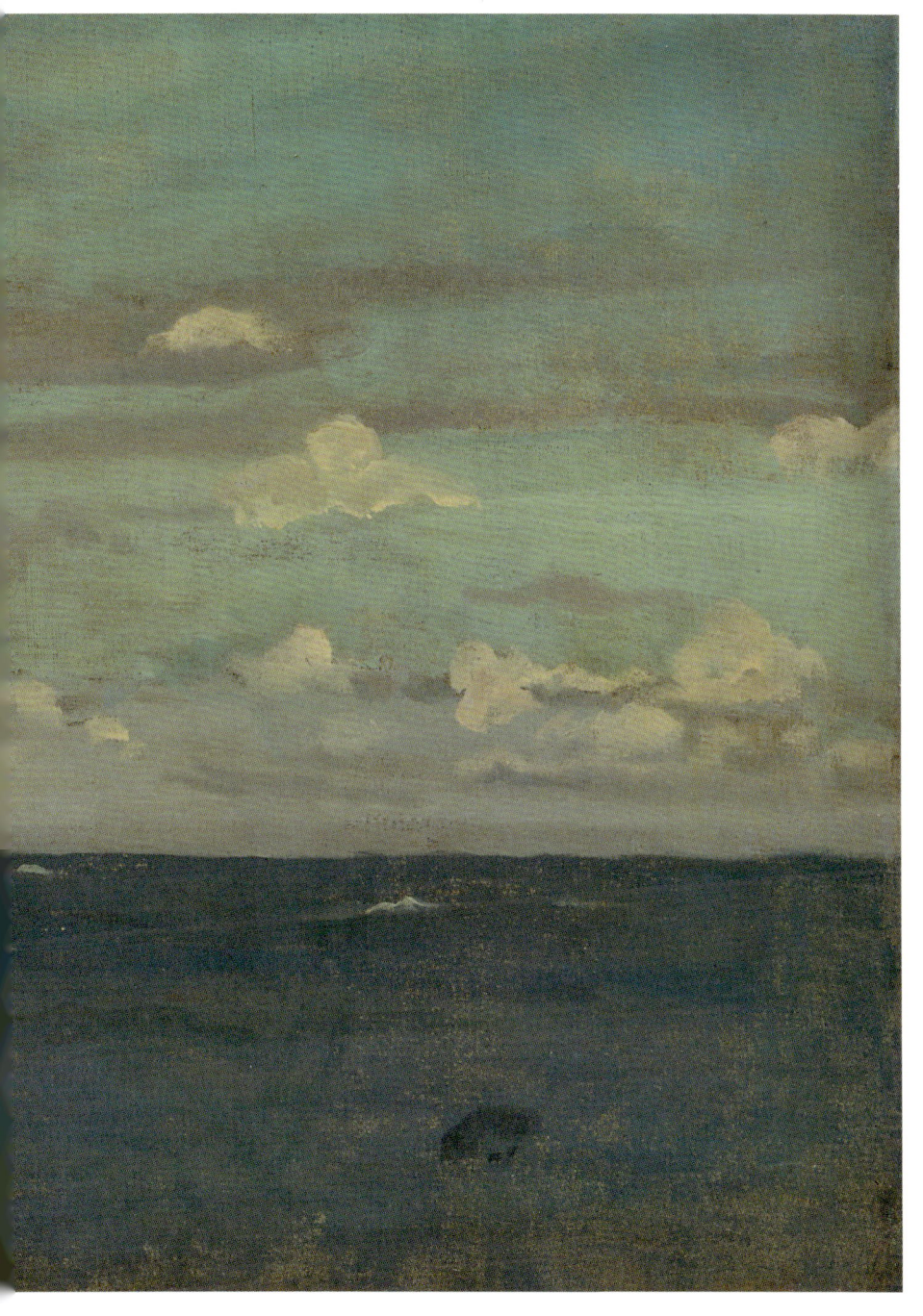

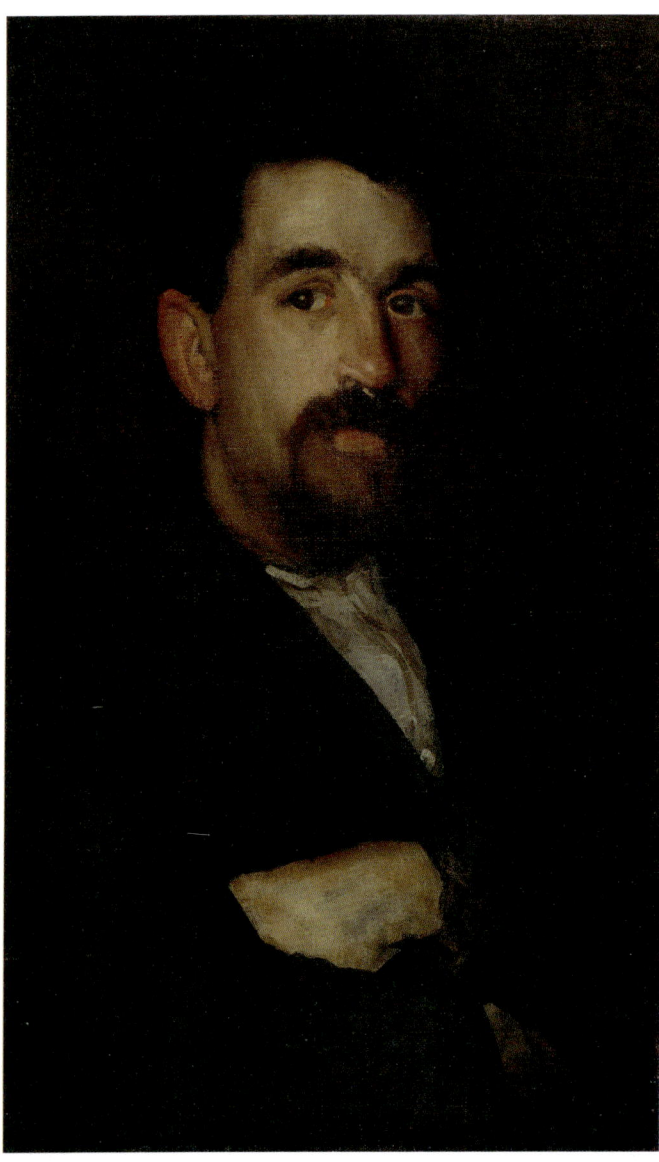

*The Master Smith of Lyme
Regis* 1895
Oil paint on canvas
51.4 × 31.1

*The Little Rose of Lyme
Regis* 1895
Oil paint on canvas
51.4 × 31.1

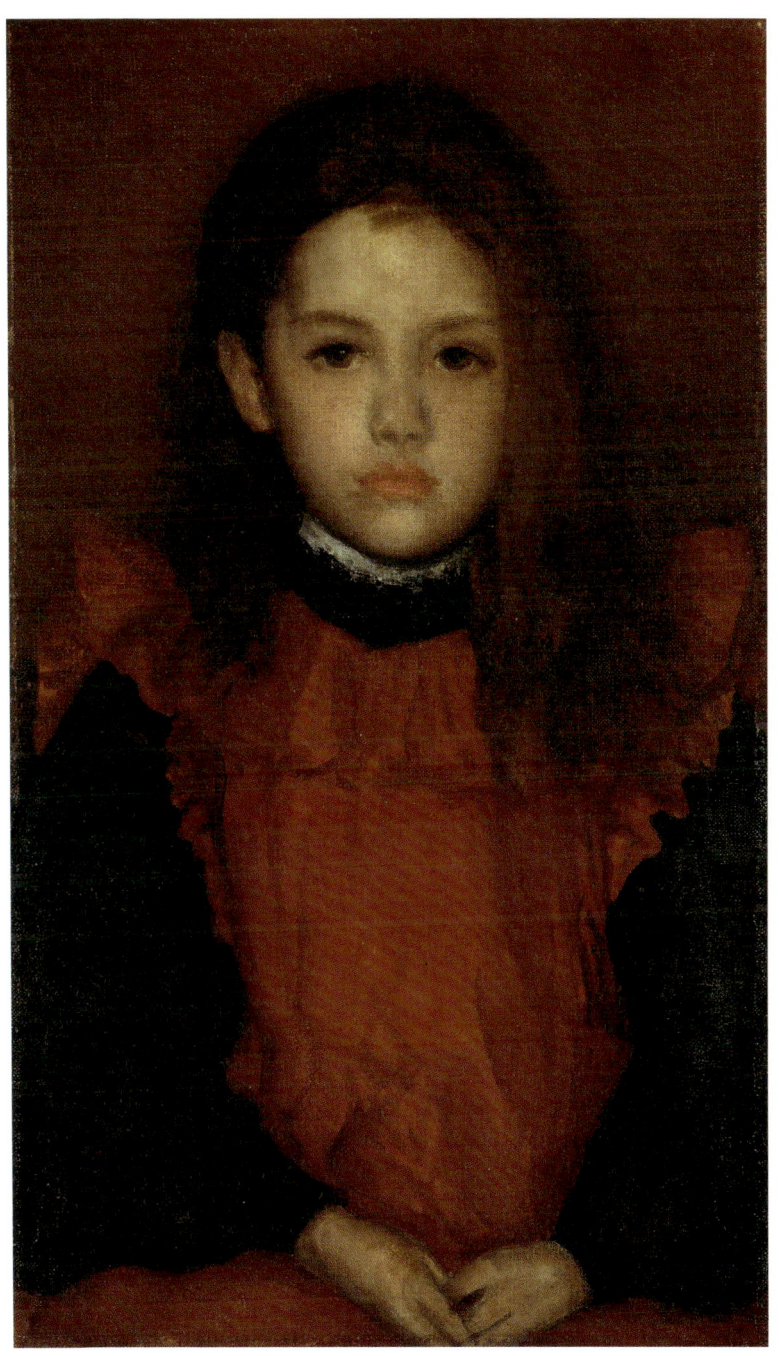

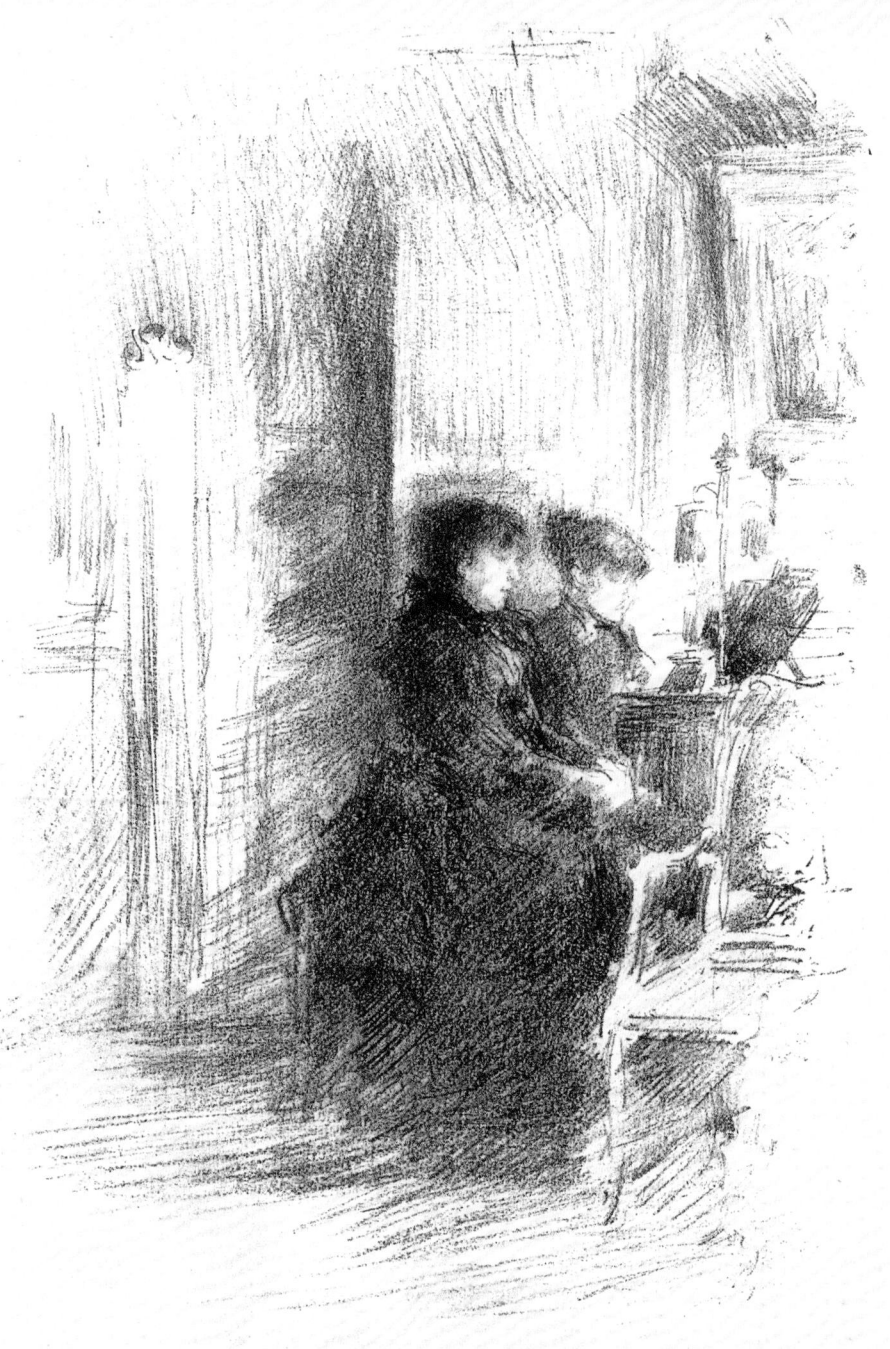

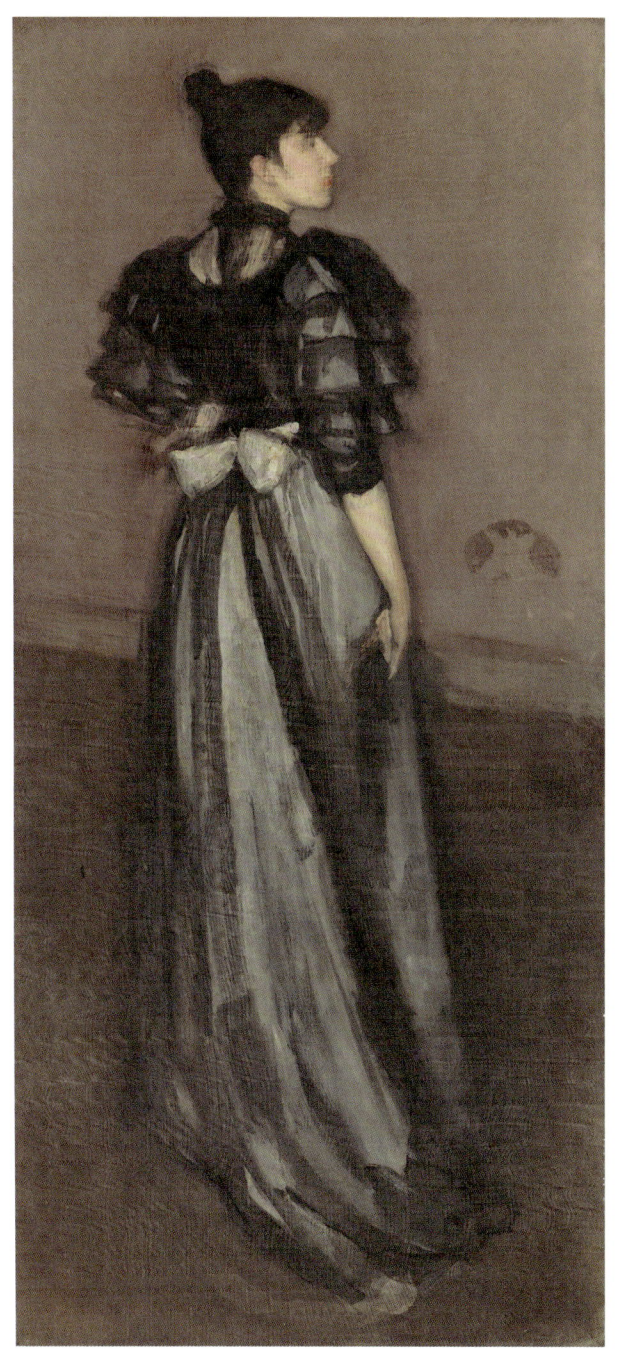

The Duet 1894
Lithograph on paper
24.6 × 16.5

Mother of Pearl and Silver:
The Andalusian 1888–1900
Oil paint on canvas
191.5 × 89.8

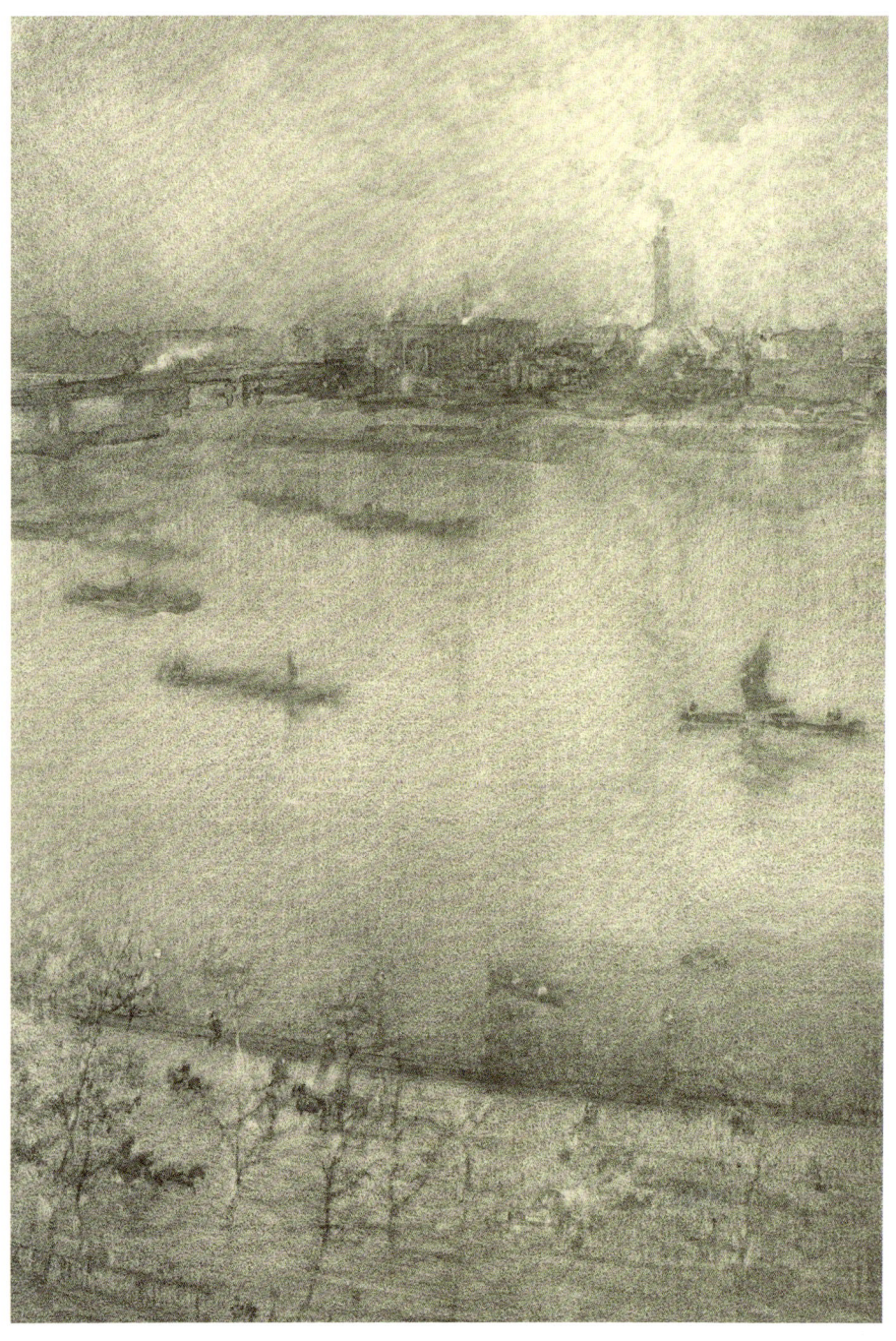

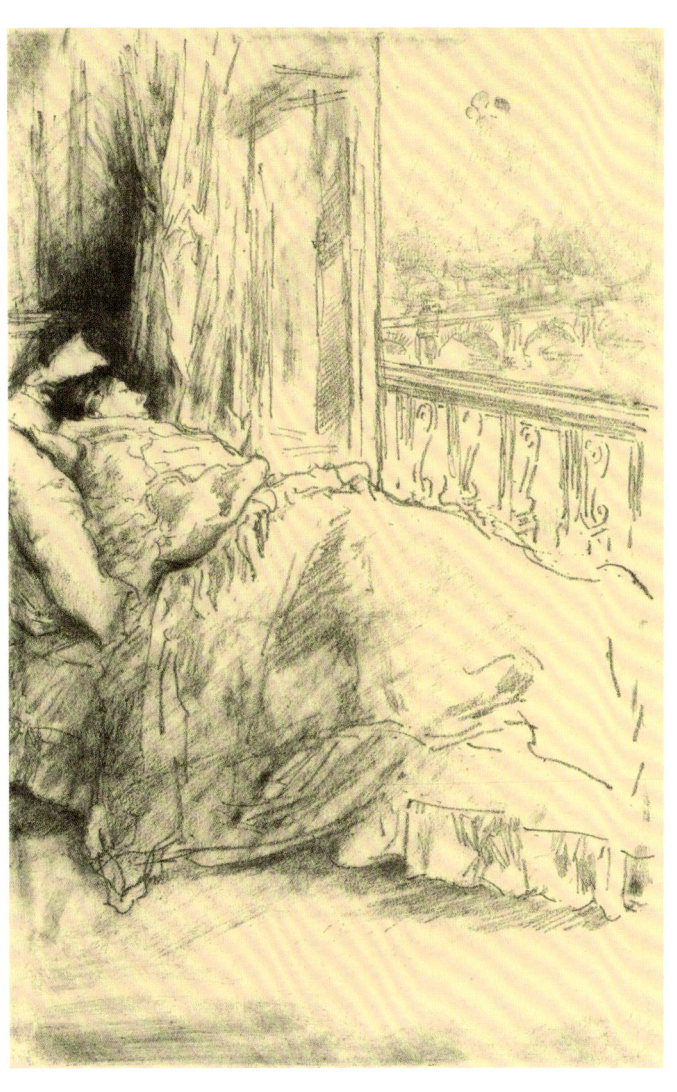

The Thames 1896
Lithotint on paper
26.7 × 19.6

By the Balcony 1896
Lithograph on paper
21.7 × 14.2

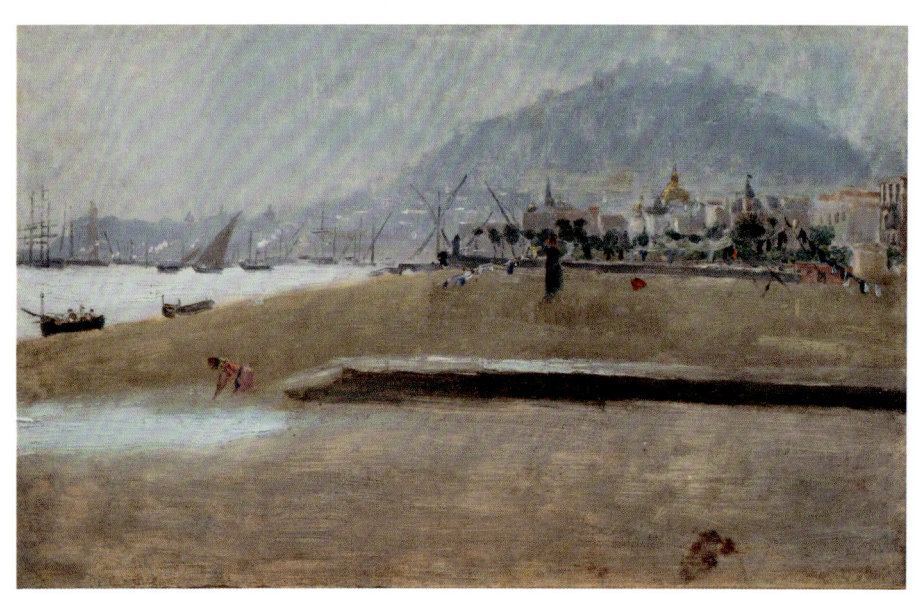

The Beach at Marseille 1901
Oil paint on wood
20.5 × 33.2

Brown and Gold 1895–1900
Oil paint on canvas
95.8 × 51.5

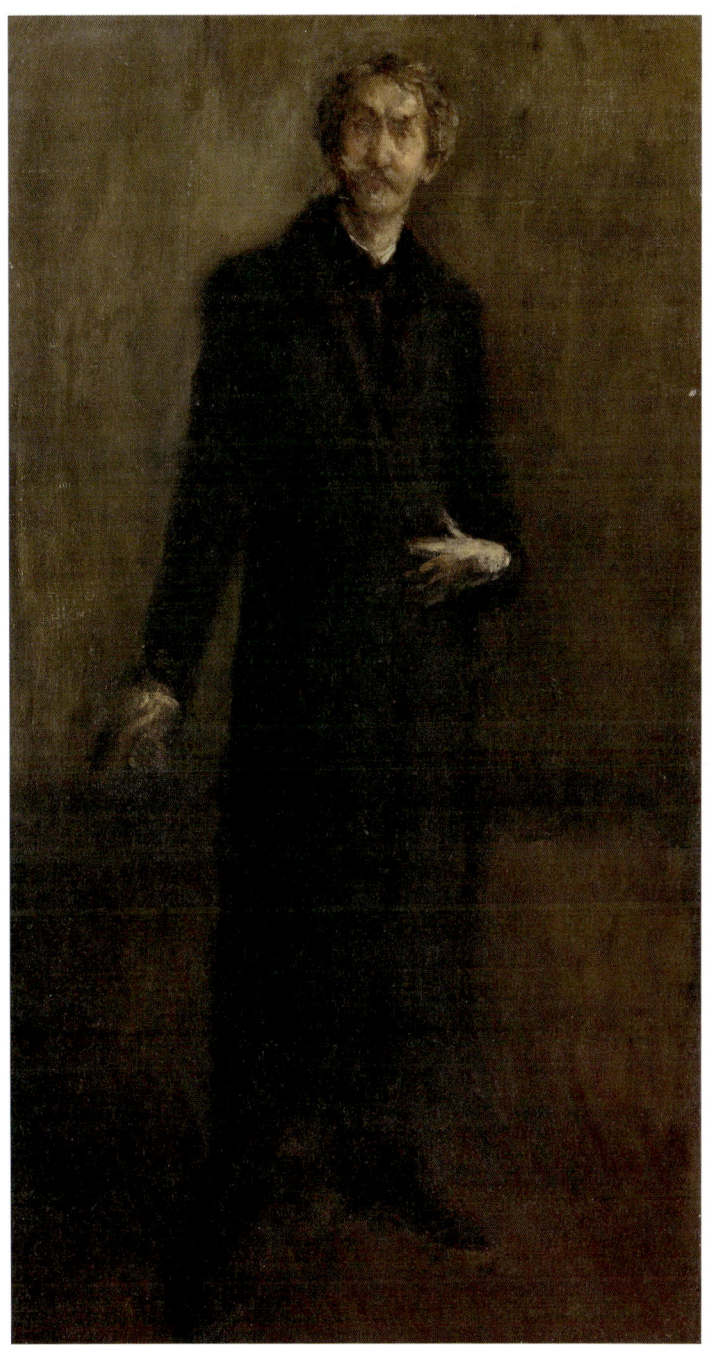

NOTES

1. Anna Matilda Whistler to Kate Palmer, 3 Nov. 1871, in Nigel Thorp (ed.), *Whistler on Art: Selected Letters and Writings of James McNeill Whistler*, Manchester 1994, p.42.

2. It was first exhibited with the title *Harmony in Blue-Green – Moonlight* and exhibited under the present title from 1879.

3. 'I can't thank you too much for the name "Nocturne" as a title for my moonlights.' Whistler to Frederick R. Leyland, Nov. 1872, in Thorp (ed.) 1994, p.46.

4. Linda Merrill, *A Pot of Paint: Aesthetics on Trial in Whistler v Ruskin*, Washington 1992, p.144.

5. Thorp (ed.) 1994, p.85.

6. Joseph and Elizabeth Pennell, *The Life of James McNeill Whistler*, London 1908, vol.1, pp.44–5.

7. Margaret F. MacDonald and Patricia de Montfort, *An American in London: Whistler and the Thames*, London 2013, p.9.

8. Daphne du Maurier (ed.), *The Young George du Maurier: A Selection of His Letters, 1860–67*, Garden City, NY 1952, p.4.

9. Nathaniel Hawthorne, *Our Old Home: A Series of English Sketches*, New York 1906, pp.283–4,

10. MacDonald and de Montfort 2013, p.18.

11. Charles Baudelaire, 'Peintres et Aquafortistes', *Le Boulevard*, 14 Sept. 1862. English translation quoted from *Copper Into Gold: Whistler and 19th-Century Printmaking*, exh. cat., Hunterian Museum, Glasgow 2003, pp.76–7. 'The Painter of Modern Life' probably dates to between November 1859 and February 1860, although it was not published until 1863. See Charles Baudelaire, *Selected Writings on Art and Literature*, trans. P.E. Charet, London 1992, p.458.

12. Whistler to Fantin-Latour, January/June 1861 (original in French), Glasgow University: Whistler (GUW) Archive, GUW 08042. For citation of this and all other GUW correspondences noted below, see the searchable resource at 'The Correspondence of James McNeill Whistler', https://www.whistler.arts.gla.ac.uk/correspondence, accessed 27 July 2024.

13. Whistler to Fantin-Latour, GUW 08042.

14. Whistler to Fantin-Latour, Sept. 1867 (original in French), GUW 08045.

15. Whistler to the *Athenaeum*, 1 July 1862, in Thorp (ed.) 1994, p.12.

16. Whistler to George Lucas, 26 June 1862, in Thorp (ed.) 1994, p.11.

17. Fantin-Latour to Whistler, 15 May 1863 (original in French), GUW 01081.

18. MacDonald and de Montfort 2013, p.23.

19. Quoted in Richard Dorment and Margaret F. MacDonald, *Whistler*, London 1994, p.78.

20. Margaret F. MacDonald in *The Woman in White: Joanna Hiffernan and James McNeill Whistler*, exh. cat., Royal Academy of Art, London and National Gallery of Art, Washington, DC 2020, p.23.

21. Whistler to Fantin-Latour, GUW 08045.

22. Dorment and MacDonald 1994, p.142.

23. Ibid., pp.164–5.

24. Ibid., p.136.

25. Ibid.

26. Whistler to Anna Matilda Whistler, March/May 1880, GUW 13502.

27. Anna Gruetzner Robins, *A Fragile Modernism: Whistler and his Impressionist Followers*, New Haven, CT 2008, p.57.

28. Whistler to Marcus Bourne Huish, 21/26 Jan. 1880, GUW 02992.

29. Camille Pissarro to Lucien Pissarro, 20 February 1883. Janine Bailly-Herzberg, *Correspondance de Camille Pissarro*, Presses Universitaires de France, Paris 1980–1991, vol.1, p.178. English translation quoted from *Copper into Gold*, exh. cat., Hunterian Museum, Glasgow 2003, p.59.

30. 'Mr Whistler's New Etchings', *Pall Mall Gazette*, 4 March 1980, p.2.

31. *James McNeill Whistler Prints*, exh. cat., Fine Art Society, London, 2016, p.105.

32. The portrait is now in the collection of the Musée d'Orsay.

33. Daniel E. Sutherland, *Whistler: A Life for Art's Sake*, New Haven, CT 2014, pp.339–40.

INDEX

Page references in *italics* indicate images.

Alexander family 21, 50
American Civil War 14
Amsterdam prints 20–1, 76–7
arrangements 14–17, 21
Arrangement en couleur chair et noir: Portrait de Théodore Duret 21, 69
Arrangement in Black, No.3: Sir Henry Irving as Philip II of Spain 21, 59
Arrangement in Black and Gold: Comte Robert de Montesquiou-Fezensac 21, 80
Arrangement in Black: Lady Meux 21, 62
Arrangement in Black: Portrait of F.R. Leyland 5, 48
Arrangement in Flesh Colour & Grey 15
Arrangement in Grey: Portrait of the Painter 16, 17
Arrangement in Grey and Black: Portrait of the Painter's Mother 13, 14, 23
Arrangement in Grey and Black, No.2: Portrait of Thomas Carlyle 21, 49
Arrangement in Yellow and Grey: Effie Deans 21, 58
At the Piano 8, 30–1
Athenaeum magazine 10

Balcony, Amsterdam 21, 76
Baudelaire, Charles 9, 10
The Beach at Marseille 23, 90
Black Lion Wharf, Wapping 14, 32
Brown and Gold 23, 91
Brown and Silver: Old Battersea Bridge 10, 34
By the Balcony 23, 89

The Canal, Amsterdam 77
Carlyle, Thomas 21, 23, 49
A Chelsea Street 71
Chinese art 10–12
The Coast of Brittany 36–7
Collins, Wilkie 10
Company of the Butterfly 23
Courbet, Gustave 6, 9
Courtyard on Canal: Grey and Red 18, 66
Cremorne Gardens, No.2 60–1
Crepuscule in Flesh Colour and Green: Valparaiso 12–13, 47

Degas, Edgar 18–20
Douze Eaux Fortes d'après Nature (or 'The French Set') 7, 7, 8

Draped Figure, Reclining 78–9
The Duet 86
Duret, Théodore 21, 23, 69

etching 6–9, 18–21

Fantin-Latour, Henri 6, 9, 10
Fine Art Society, London 18, 20
Franklin, Maud 18, 21, 58
Freer, Charles 17
'The French Set' 7, 7, 8
Fry, Roger 23

The Gentle Art of Making Enemies (writings) 18
Gershwin, George 5
Gleyre, Charles 6
Godwin, Beatrice (wife) 21, 22, 23
Godwin, Edward W. 18
Goupil Gallery, London 23
Greaves, Henry and Walter 5

Haden, Deborah (née Whistler, half-sister) 7, 8, 9, 30–1
Haden, Francis Seymour 7–8, 9, 13–14
Harmony in Blue and Gold: The Peacock Room 15, 15–17
Harmony in Blue and Silver: Trouville 46
Harmony in Flesh Colour and Black: Portrait of Mrs Louise Jopling 63
Harmony in Grey and Green: Miss Cicely Alexander 21, 50
Harmony in Red: Lamplight 21, 22
Hawthorne, Nathaniel 8
Hiffernan, Joanna 8, 10–12, 11, 39–42
Hiroshige, Utagawa 12
Hogarth, William 23
Hôtel de Ville, Loches 74

Imperial Academy of Fine Arts, St Petersburg 6
interior design projects 15, 15–17
Irving, Sir Henry 21, 59

Japanese art 10–12
John, Gwen 23
Jones, Milly 12, 40–1
Jopling, Louise 63

The Last of Old Westminster 10, 35
Legros, Alphonse 6
Leyland, Frances 51

Leyland, Frederick Richards 5, 12, 15–17, 21, 48
The Lime-Burner 9, 33
lithography 23
The Little Rose of Lyme Regis 23, 85
The Little Venice 20, 65
The Long Balcony 75

Mallarmé, Stéphane 18, 23, 81
The Master Smith of Lyme Regis 23, 84
La Mère Gérard 27
Meux, Lady 21, 62
Millais, John Everett 8
Montesquiou-Fezensac, Robert de 21, 80
Mother of Pearl and Silver: The Andalusian 23, 87
Musée du Luxembourg, Paris 23
musical terminology 5
The Music Room 29

nocturnes 5–6
Nocturne 23, 64
Nocturne: Black and Gold – The Fire Wheel 56
Nocturne: Blue and Gold – Battersea Bridge 55
Nocturne: Blue and Gold – Southampton Water 54
Nocturne: Blue and Silver – Chelsea 4, 5
Nocturne: Blue and Silver – Cremorne Lights 52–3
Nocturne in Black and Gold: The Falling Rocket 17, 57
Nocturne: Palaces 19, 20

Pater, Walter 5
Pissarro, Camille 20
portraiture 21–3
La Princesse du Pays de la Porcelaine 17, 43
printmaking *see* etching; lithography
Purple and Rose: The Lange Leizen of the Six Marks 12, 42

Quilter, Harry 18

A Red Note: Fête on the Sands, Ostend 72
Rossetti, Dante Gabriel 12
Rossi, Carmen 23
Royal Academy 8, 10, 12, 14, 15
Ruskin, John 17–18

St Ives 70

Salon des Refusés, Paris 10
Scott, Walter 21
The Sea, Pourville 24–5
self-portraiture 16, 17, 23, 91
*A Series of Sixteen Etchings of
    Scenes on the Thames* (or
    'The Thames Set') 8–9,
    21, 23, 88–9
Shaw, George Bernard 21
Sickert, Walter 20
*Sketch of the Interior of the
    Suffolk Street Gallery during
    an Exhibition* 15, 73
*Sketches on the Coast Survey
    Plate* 6, 26
Société des Trois 6
Society of British Artists
    15, 73
Stéphane Mallarmé 18, 81
Street at Saverne 28
Swinburne, Algernon 12
*Symphony in Flesh Colour
    and Pink: Portrait of Mrs
    Frances Leyland* 51
*Symphony in White, No.1:
    The White Girl* 10, 11
*Symphony in White, No.2: The
    Little White Girl* 10–12, 39
Symphony in White, No.3
    12, 40–1

'10 O'Clock' (lecture) 18
The Thames 23, 88
'The Thames Set' 8–9, 21,
    23, 88–9
Three Figures: Pink and Grey 45

Vanderbilt, George W. 21
*Variations in Flesh Colour and
    Green: The Balcony* 44
Venice print sets 18–21,
    19, 66
Violet and Silver: A Deep Sea
    82–3

Wapping 8, 9, 10
Weary 38
Whibley, Ethel (née Philip,
    sister-in-law) 23, 87
Whistler, Anna Matilda
    (née McNeill, mother) 5,
    6, 13, 14, 23
Whistler, Beatrice (Godwin,
    wife) 21, 22, 23
Whistler, James McNeill
    bankruptcy 18, 21
    in Chile 12–13
    early years 6–8
    exhibitions 14–15, 23
    family 12–14
    final years 23
    and Glasgow 23
    libel case 17–18

in London 5–6, 7–10,
    13–14, 23
in Lyme Regis 23
materials and
    techniques 5, 18–20
in Paris 6–7, 10, 23
partners 10–12, 21, 23
personality 17–18
in Russia 6
in Venice 18–21
Whistler, Major George
    Washington (father) 6
Whistler, William (brother)
    13–14
*Whistler v. Ruskin: Art & Art
    Critics* (pamphlet) 17
White House, Tite Street,
    London 18, 21
Wilde, Oscar 18

The Yellow Room 68

*The Zattere: Harmony in Blue
    and Brown* 18, 67

CREDITS

First published 2024 by order of the Tate Trustees
by Tate Publishing, a division of Tate Enterprises Ltd
Millbank, London SW1P 4RG
www.tate.org.uk/publishing

A catalogue record for this book is available from
the British Library

ISBN 978 1 84976 952 5

Distributed in the United States and Canada by
ABRAMS, New York

Library of Congress Control Number applied for

Commissioning Editor: Emma Poulter
Editorial Assistant: Aki Gurung
Production: Juliette Dupire
Picture Researcher: Emma O'Neill
Design: Astrid Stavro Studio
Colour reproduction by DL Imaging, London
Printed and bound in Italy by Printer Trento S.r.l

Cover: *Nocturne: Blue and Silver – Cremorne Lights*
1872 (detail, see pp.52–3)
Frontispiece: *Symphony in White, No.2: The Little
White Girl* 1864 (detail, see p.39)

Measurements of artworks are given in
centimetres, height before width and depth

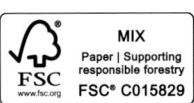

THE AUTHOR
James Finch is a curator and art historian
specialising in British art of the nineteenth and
twentieth centuries. He is currently Assistant
Curator, Nineteenth-Century British Art at Tate
Britain where he curated the exhibition *Sargent
and Fashion* and co-curated *The Rossettis* and *Turner's
Modern World*. Prior to joining Tate, James was
Curatorial Assistant at the Royal Academy of
Arts, London, and undertook his doctorate, as a
partnership between the University of Kent and
Tate. He has published widely on nineteenth-
and twentieth-century art.